DICTIONARY OF PROVERBS

Neil Wilson

PENTAGON PRESS
DELHI INDIA

Dictionary of Proverbs

Neil Wilson

All rights reserved. No part of this publication may be copied, reproduced, stored in a retrieval system or transmitted in any form or by any means without specific prior permission of the publisher.

First Published: 2004
Revised: 2006

© Reserved

ISBN 81-86830-94-4

PENTAGON PRESS
A-38, Hauz Khas, New Delhi-110016 (India)
Phones: 011-51656996/7/8 • Tele-fax: 011-51656997
E-mail: pentagonpress@touchtelindia.net
www.pentagon-press.com

Sale Office :
Flat # 105, 106, 4262, St. # 3
Ansari Road, Darya Ganj, Delhi-110002.

Printed at New Elegant Printers, New Delhi.

CONTENTS

A 5
B 11
C 19
D 31
E 39
F 49
G 58
H 65
I 76
J 79
K 81
L 83
M 91
N 104
O 107
P 109
Q 125
R 127
S 134

T	151
U	160
V	163
W	167
Y	177
Z	178
Famous Proverbs	179
Modern Proverbs	192
Famous Lines Of Leaders	194
Ideas Of Great Authors	200
More Proverbs	214
Miscellaneous	225
Exercise:	237

A

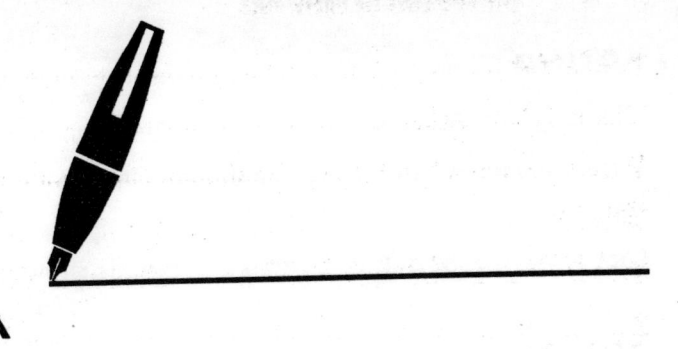

ABILITY

Behind an able man, there are always other able men.

They are able, because they think they are able.

Ability is of little account without opportunity.

ABSENCE

Absence makes the heart grow fonder.

Love reckons hours for months and days for years and every little absence is an age.

Out of sight, out of mind.

ACQUAINTANCE

Familiarity breeds contempt.

Sudden acquaintance brings repentance.

If a man is worth knowing at all, he is worth knowing well.

ACTING

The play's the thing.

When an actor has money, he doesn't send letters, but telegrams.

One who cannot dance, blames the dancing courtyard.

ACTION

Strong reasons make strong action.

He who thinks without doing, is as great a fool as he who does, without thinking.

Let us do or die.

Better wear out than rust out.

Do well and right and let the whole world sink.

An idle mind is a devil's workshop.

Learn to labour and to wait.

What's done can't be undone.

Their's is not to make reply,

Their's is not to reason why,

Their's is but to do and die.

ADAM

Oh, Adam was a gardener.

Adam ate the apple and our teeth still ache.

In Adam's fall, we sinned all.

Whilst Adam slept: Eve from his side arose,
Strange his first sleep, would be his last repose.

ADMIRATION

Distance is a great promoter of admiration.

Fools favour flattery; flattery favours fools.

ADVERSITY

A poor man has no friend.

A friend in need is a friend indeed.

If you want to know the value of money, go and borrow some.

Sweet are the uses of adversity.

What I crave for is poverty.

There is no education like adversity.

We stoop to conquer.

Let me embrace thee, sour adversity.

Great men rejoice in adversity as brave soldiers triumph in war.

Everybody praises his articles.

Even truth needs to be advertised.

ADVICE

Never give advice in a crowd.

Whatever advice you give, be brief.

It is not good to advice everybody.

Never advise anyone to go to war or to marry.

Advice is offensive-it shows us that we are known to others as well as to ourselves.

Many receive advice, only the wise profit by it.

The worst men often give the best advice.

AFFLICTION

Whom the Lord loveth, he chastiseth.

Sweet are the uses of adversity.

Bitters of life, like Amla, have sweet after-taste.

When bitter becomes bitterest, it becomes a bit rest.

What cannot be cured must be endured.

Desperate maladies need desperate remedies.

AGE

An old man is twice a child.

Old men and children are alike.

AGRICULTURE

Hope sustains the husbandman.

Earth is here so kind, that just tickle her with a hoe and she laughs with harvest.

ANCESTRY

An ass does know its ancestors.

Breed is more vital than birth.

Noble ancestry makes a poor dish at table.

Whoever serves his country well, has no need of ancestors.

ANGER

Be swift to hear, slower to speak, still slower to wrath.

An angry man is an ill man.

Never answer a letter, while you are angry.

Anger is a kind of temporary madness.

When angry, count ten.

Beware the fury of a patient man.

APPEARANCE

All that glitters is not gold.

Say and pose what you are, but look forward always to achieve greater goal.

Appearances are deceptive.

AMBITION

Hitch your wagon to a star.

Ambition destroys its possessor.

If you wish to reach the highest, start at the lowest.

The desire of power in excess caused man to fall.

The desire of knowledge in excess caused man to fall.

ANIMALS

Men today are worse than animals.

Men show their superiority inside; animals outside.

ART

Art is life, seen through a temperament.

High instincts before which our moral nature did tremble like a guilty thing surprised.

BEAUTY

A thing of beauty is a joy forever.

Beauty is worse than wine; it intoxicates both the holder and the beholder.

Everything has its beauty, but not everyone sees it.

Beauty is in the eye of the beholder.

Beauty is truth, truth is beauty.

Beauty is everlasting.

Youth is happy because it has the ability to see beauty.

Beauty provoketh thieves sooner than gold.

There is no cosmetic for beauty like happiness.

Beauty is but skin-deep.

Beauty is potent but money is omnipotent.

Beauty will buy no beef.

BEGGING

Beggars must not be choosers.

Borrowing is not better than begging.

If you want to know the value of money, go and try to beg some.

If wishes were horses, beggars would ride.

He who begs timidly courts refusal.

BEGINNING

Well begun is half done.

It is the beginning of the end.

Begin today, end never.

A good beginning makes a good ending.

It is always morning somewhere in the world.

It is only the first step, which is troublesome.

It is the beginning of the end.

BELIEF

Those who have eyes to see may see,

Those who have ears to hear may hear.

Men willingly believe what they wish.

He that believeth not shall be damned.

Nothing is so firmly believed as what we least know.

Belief has need of the whole truth.

Belief without work is dead.

BENEFIT

If you confer a benefit, never remember it, if you receive one, never forget it.

BIBLE

The Bible is a window in this prison-world.

BIOGRAPHY

Biography is the only true history.

Biography is the most universally pleasant and profitable of all reading.

The best teachers of humanity are the lives of great men.

BIRDS

A bird in hand is worth two in the bush.

Birds of a feather flock together.

Life-breath is a bird.

The bird a nest, the spider a web, man friendship.

Thou was not born for death, immortal Bird!

Better an egg today than a hen tomorrow.

BIRTH

The sun that rises on earth sets in heaven.

(i.e. when we are born on earth, we die in heaven).

Human birth is rare and difficult.

Pray for us now and at the hour of our birth.

Prevention of birth is a precipitation of murder.

BLESSING

Blessings never come in pairs; misfortunes never come alone.

God blesses everyone.

BLINDNESS

In the kingdom of the blind, one-eyed man is king.

(Andhon main kana raja.)

The blind Town ruled by a King Fool.

A blind cannot judge colours.

If the blind lead the blind, both shall fall into a ditch.

There's none so blind as they that won't see.

Run away from a fool; you cannot teach him.

Where there is no vision, the people perish.

BLOOD

Blood is thicker than water.

Water is thinner than blood.

The blood of the martyrs is the seed of the church.

Blood alone moves the history of destiny.

BODY

Your body is the temple of the Holy Ghost.

A sound mind in a healthy body.

Body is a cage of bones in which the soul dwells like a bird.

We are bound to our bodies like an oyster to its shell.

If anything is sacred, human body is sacred.

BOOKS

Laws die, books never.

Beware of the man of one book.

No furniture is so charming as books, even if you never open them or read a single word.

A book is like a garden carried in the pocket.

A best seller is the gilded tomb of a mediocre talent.

If you throw a handful of jewels inside the head of a man, nobody can take it away.

A book may be as great a thing as a battle.

A book is somehow sacred.

Books without the knowledge of life are useless.

BORE

Bore: one who is interesting to a point - the point of departure.

A bore is a person who takes his time taking your time.

The secret of being a bore is to tell everything.

The biggest bore is the person who is bored by everyone and everything.

BOY

One boy is more trouble than a dozen girls.

Boys will be boys.

BREAD

When there is no bread in the stomach, everything goes wrong.

Bread is the staff of life.

Man does not live by bread alone.

Give us this day our daily bread.

A wise man does not quarrel with his bread and butter.

Be true to your salt.

Half a loaf is better than no bread.

BRAVERY

None but the brave deserve the fair.

Cowards die many times,
The brave die but once.
The brave will save.
Boldness is a mask for fear, however great.
A man can die, but once.

BREVITY

Brevity is the soul of wit.
The fewer the words, the better the prayer.
The more the people talk, the less they think.
The more you say, the less the people remember.

BRIBERY

Every man hath his price.
Few men have virtue to withstand the highest bidder.

BROTHERHOOD

Am I my brother's keeper?
Liberty! equality! fraternity!
A brother is a friend given by nature.
Brothers are brothers evermore.

BRUSH

Don't be ruffled if now and then you get a brush from the world; it will be over in no time and everything will be all right.

BUSINESS

Business like our automobile has to be driven in order to get results.

The British are a nation of shopkeepers.

The nature of business is swindling.

The business of America is business.

Do not kill the hen that lays golden eggs.

Few people do business well, who do nothing else.

No nation was ever ruined by business.

Business is business.

Everybody's business is nobody's business.

C

CARE

Care kills the cat.

I am sure, care's an enemy to life.

To carry care to bed is to sleep with a pack on your back.

The wife of a careless man is always a widow.

CAT

When the cat's away, the mice will play.

Curiosity kills the cat.

There is no room to swing a cat.

Even a cat is a lion in her own house.

It is not worthwhile to go round the world to count the bats in Zanzibar.

A cat has nine lives.

The cat would eat fish, but would not wet her feet.

CAUTION

Precaution is better than cure.

Hasten slowly.

Be slow of tongue and quick of eye.

When buying use your eyes rather than your ears.

The cautious seldom err.

Little boats should keep near shore.

Drink nothing without seeing, sign nothing without reading it.

Pitchers have ears.

CENSURE

Censure is the tax a man pays to the public for being maintained.

CERTAIN

In this world, nothing is certain, but death and taxes.

CHANGE

Never swap horses midstream.

Long live the revolution!

Change is the law of nature.

Everything changes but change.

The old order changeth, yielding place to the new.

Things do not change; we change.

We die and are reborn as we change our clothes.

CHARACTER

When wealth is lost, nothing is lost;

When health is lost, something is lost;

When character is lost, everything is lost.

Character is what you are in the dark.

Integrity in speech and deed is the backbone of character.

Slow and steady wins the race.

Look before you leap.

To have two strings to one's bow.

In fair weather, prepare for foul.

Walls have ears.

Let not thy left hand know what thy right hand doeth.

Among mortals, second thoughts are wisest.

Beware of the young doctor and the young barber.

He that cannot see well, let him go softly.

Fair and softly goes far in a day.

Hear all men speak, but credit few or none.

CHARITY

Charity begins at home.

Let charity begin at home, but end abroad.

Charity shall cover a multitude of sins.

Condemn the fault, not the actor of it.

With malice towards none; with charity for all...

Charity deals with symptoms instead of causes.

Every charitable act is a stepping-stone towards heaven.

Charity is the virtue of the heart and not the hand.

Charity begins at home and is the voice of the world.

Charity creates a multitude of sins.

CHEERFULNESS

He who sings frightens away his ills.

A laugh a day will keep illness away.

Cheer up, the worst is yet to be.

My religion of life is always to be cheerful.

A cheerful face is nearly as good for an invalid as healthy weather.

A good laugh is sunshine in the house.

All succeeds with people who are sweet and cheerful.

CHILDREN

Spare the rod and spoil the child.

The child is the father of the man.

A wise son maketh a glad father.

In the child, the father's image lies.

If children grew up according to early indications, we should have nothing but geniuses.

The future destiny of the child is always the work of the mother.

Children many tear up a house, but they never break up a house.

Heaven lies about us in our infancy.

Life's aspirations come in the guise of children.

CHOICE

There is small choice in rotten apples.

Beggars are not choosers.

For many are called but few are chosen.

CHOOSING

You cannot make an omlette without breaking eggs.

Choose neither woman nor linen by candle-light.

You have freedom of choice, but not freedom from choice.

You cannot eat your cake and have it.

The difficulty in life is the choice.

Sometimes it is a good choice not to choose at all.

CHRIST

Jesus Christ is the same yesterday, today, forever.

CIRCUMSTANCES

Circumstances alter cases.

Adapt circumstances to yourself or adapt yourself to circumstances.

CITY

God made the country, man made the town.

The people are the city.

CLEANLINESS

Cleanliness is next to godliness.

God loveth the clean.

CLEVERNESS

The clever are like crows; they eat dirt.

Cleverness is not wisdom.

CLOTHES

Clothes make the man.

COLOURS

Blue is true.
Yellow's jealous.
Green's forsaken
Red's brazen
White is love.
And Black is death.

COMMUNISM

From each according to his ability to each according to his needs.

COMPANY

Two's company, three's crowd.
A man is known by the company he keeps.

COMPARISON

Judge not that you be not judged.
Comparisons are odious.

COMPENSATION

The prickly thorn often bears roses.

COMPROMISE

Better bend than break.

To run with the hare and hunt with the hounds.

CONFESSION

Open confession is good for the soul.

One who tells all he knows will also tell what he does not.

God forgives those who sincerely confess.

CONCEIT

Seest thou a man wise in his conceit? There is more hope of a fool than of him.

Pride goes before a fall.

The head of haughtiness will hang down.

COMPLAINING

Those who do not complain are never pitied.

COMPLIMENT

Compliments are only lies in court clothes.

A compliment is something like a kiss through a veil.

CONFIDENCE

Be courteous to all, but intimate with few.

Blind belief is better than no belief.

Skill and confidence are an unconquered army.

Confidence carries conviction.

Society is built upon trust.

CONQUEST

To rejoice in conquest is to rejoice in murder.

How grand is victory, but how dear!

Self-conquest is the greatest of victories.

CONSCIENCE

There is no pillow so soft as a clean conscience.

Conscience is God's presence in man.

CONSISTENCY

Shoemaker, stick to your last

CONTENTMENT

He is well paid who is well satisfied.

CONVERSATION

The less men know, the more they talk.

Silence is one great art of conversation.

Speech is silver, silence is gold.

Talk less, think more.

CORRUPTION

The more corrupt the State, the more the laws.

A foolish king rules over a city of the blind.

COURAGE

A man of courage is also a man of faith.

The courage we desire and prize is not the courage to die decently, but to live, manfully.

Fortune and love befriend the bold.

COOKING

Too many cooks spoil the broth.

God sends meat and the devil sends cooks.

The proof of the pudding is in the eating.

You cannot both eat your cake and have it.

COURTESY

Courtesy pays.

The small courtesies sweeten life.

A coward is incapable of exhibiting love; it is the prerogative of the brave.

CRAZE

Of all odd crazes, the craze to be forever reading new books is one of the oddest.

CREDULITY

Better be too credulous than too sceptic.

He who never questions, never learns.

Credulity is man's weakness, but child's strength.

Trust everybody until he proves untrustworthy.

Trust begets trust.

CREDIT

In God we trust; all others must pay cash.

No man's credit is as good as his money.

CUSTOM

Other times, other customs.

Ancient custom has the force of law.

Custom is often only the antiquity of error.

While in Rome, do as the Romans do.

Custom is the Universal Sovereign.

CRIME

One crime is everything, two nothing.

Murder will be out.

It is not the thief who is hanged, but one who is caught stealing.

As well be hanged for a cow as for a hen.

CRITICISM

Judge not, lest you be not judged.

Even a lion had to defend himself against lies.

Said the pot to the kettle, 'Get away, blackface.'

CRUELTY

I must be cruel only to be kind.

CULTURE

Culture ends in headache.

Culture is gilt, not gold.

CURIOSITY

Curiosity killed the cat.

Ask me no questions and I'll tell you no fibs.

D

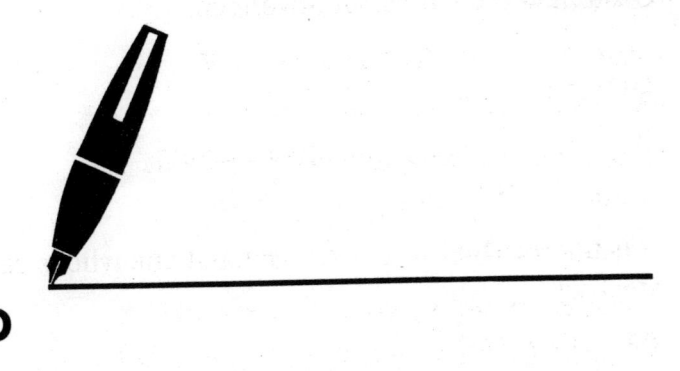

DANGER

Danger is the spice of life.

Though a man can escape every other danger, he can never wholly escape those who do not want such a person as he is to exist.

We are in most danger when we think ourselves to be the safest.

The pitcher that goes too often in the well is broken at last.

Danger is never overcome without danger.

A danger foreseen is half avoided.

Never was anything great achieved without danger.

Danger for danger's sake is senseless.

The danger past and God forgotten.

DARING

Who that never climbed never fell.

Who dares nothing, needs hope for nothing.

Heaven helps those who help themselves.

DARKNESS

It is always darkest just before the dawn.

When it is dark, it is a sign of coming light.

O darkness! thou hast beauties as the morn.

DAUGHTER

A daughter is an embarrassing and ticklish possession.

A son is a son till he gets his wife. A daughter is a daughter all her life.

DAY

You have spent the night in sleeping and the day in eating and thus wasted your jewels like life.

One glance of thine creates a day.

What a day may bring, a day may take away.

Boast not thyself of tomorrow, for thou knowest not what a day may bring forth.

DEATH

Heaven gives its favourites early death.

In the midst of life we are in death.

Yet a little sleep, a little slumber, a little folding of the hands to sleep.

Death comes to all.

The goal of all life is death.

There is no death, only a change of worlds.

A man can die, but once we owe God a death.

Call no man happy till he is dead.

Death is a thing of grandeur.

God's finger touched him and he slept.

Death is the golden key that opens the palace of eternity.

DEBT

Debt is the worst poverty.

Debt is a bottomless sea.

Once in debt, always in debt.

Debt is a great cobweb.

Borrowing is sorrowing.

Neither a borrower nor a lender be.

For loan loses both itself and friend.

Debt is the worst poverty.

The second vice is lying; the first is running into debt.

Debt is the prolific mother of folly and of crime.

DECAY

A man is like a tree: he dies on top first.

DECENCY

Decency is indecency's conspiracy of silence.

DECEPTION

All warfare is based on deception.
It is double pleasure to deceive the deceiver.

DEDICATION

Give your life to none, I say, save to him who gave it.

DEEDS

I am a man of deeds, I have no time for learning.
Noble deeds that are concealed are most esteemed.
Begin not with a programme, but with a deed.
Give me the ready hand rather than the ready tongue.
Small deeds done are better than great deeds planned.
The smallest deed is better than the grandest intention.

DELAY

Delay is ever fatal to those who are prepared.
Better late than never.

DEMOCRACY

The world must be made safe for democracy.

Democracy is a government of the people, by the people, for the people.

It is far better to rule by love than fear.

DESIRE

First desire, then acquire.

He who desires nothing will be free.

Desire is the very essence of man.

First deserve, then desire.

All human activity is prompted by desire.

We soon believe what we desire.

He who desires not will always be free.

DESPAIR

All hope abandon ye who enter here.

Despair doubles our strength.

Despair ruins some, presumption many.

DESTINY

Every man meets his Waterloo at last.

DEVIL

Think of the devil and there he is.

The prince of darkness is a gentleman.

Give the devil his due.

The devil can quote the scripture for his purpose.

DIPLOMACY

A diplomat is a man who knows his lady's birthday, but does not know her age.

When a diplomat says, "Yes," he means "Perhaps".

When he says 'Perhaps", he means "No", when he says "No", he is no diplomat.

DISAPPOINTMENT

How disappointment tracks the steps of hope.

Disappointment is the nurse of wisdom.

DISCONTENTMENT

Discontentment is true misery.

Discontentment is the cause of all progress.

DISCRETION

Discretion is the better part of valour.

An ounce of discretion is worth a pound of wit.

DISEASE

What cannot be cured must be endured.

Every disease is the symptom of a greater disease.

Desperate diseases require desperate remedies.

DISGRACE

No one can disgrace us, but ourselves.

DISTANCE

Distance lends enchantment to the view.

DOG

A hungry dog fights best.

Every dog has its day.

Give a dog bad name and hang him.

Let the sleeping dogs lie.

Every dog is entitled to its bite.

When a man bites a dog, it is news.

DOUBT

Our doubts are traitors.

Doubt destroys deeds.

Who knows most, doubts not.

When in doubt, win the trick.

DREAM

We are such stuff as dreams are made of.

DRESS

Clothes make a man.

Eat to please yourself, but dress to please others.

It is only fine feathers that make fine birds.

DUTY

The dutiful are beautiful.

There is not a moment without some duty.

Do the duty that lies nearest to thee.

Duty is the royal talisman; duty alone will lead to the goal.

Truth is a divine word.
Duty is a divine law.

Duty is what one expects from others.

When duty calls, some people are never at home.

Duty determines destiny.

The path of duty was the way to glory.

E

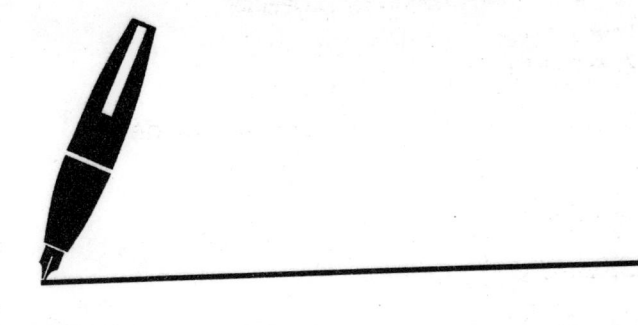

EARLY

Early to bed and early to rise, makes a man healthy, wealthy and wise.

When one begins to turn in bed, it is time to turn out.

The early morning hath gold in its mouth.

Better early than late.

EARNESTNESS

Earnestness is enthusiasm tempered by reason.

A man in earnest finds means, or if he cannot, creates them.

EATING

The proof of pudding is in the eating.

Eat to live, not live to eat.

Eat, drink and be merry for tomorrow we die.

The nearer the bone, the sweeter the meat.

Unless there is bread in the stomach, everything goes away.

A cheerful look makes a feast.

The way to a man's heart is through his stomach.

Bread is the staff of life.

Eat to please thyself; dress to please others.

ECONOMY

He who will not economise,
Will have to agonise.

Penny wise, pound foolish.

EDUCATION

If you put a handful of pearls in the head of a child, he cannot be robbed of them.

Let us mend our education or end our education.

Each one, teach one. Each alive, teach five.

True education is not a purchasable commodity; it cannot be bought and sold.

Learn to teach; teach to learn.

Learn to live before you live to learn.

Learn by earning; earn by learning.

There is no education like adversity.

Education has for its object the formation of character.

Education makes people easy to lead, but difficult to drive.

Education is freedom.

Education is discipline for the adventure of life.

The highest result of education is toleration.

Education is the apprenticeship of life.

EFFICIENCY

The best carpenters make the fewest chips.

What is worth doing is worth doing well.

Do not put all your eggs in one basket.

EGOTIST

Egotist is one who is always deep in conversation.

An egotist always hurts the person he loves-himself.

EGOTISM

Nothing is more to me than myself.

ELOQUENCE

It is the spoken word that rules the world.

Thoughts that breath and words that burn.

Eloquence may exist without a proportionable degree of wisdom.

Brevity is a great charm of eloquence.

Eloquence is the poetry of prose.

END

The end must justify the means.

The rest is silence.

He laughs best that laughs last.

Better the last smile than the first laughter.

All is well that ends well.

Let the end try the man.

ENEMY

A wise enemy is better than a foolish friend.

Do not underrate your enemy.

Be careful in the choice of your enemies.

Man is his own worst enemy.

They love him most for the enemies that he had made.

A man cannot be too careful in the choice of his enemies.

Our enemies are our outward consciences.

Observe your enemies for they first find out your faults.

There is no little enemy.

He that is not with me is against me.

Take heed of a reconciled enemy.

ENERGY

The truest wisdom, in general, is a resolute determination.

He alone has energy who cannot be deprived of it.

This world belongs to the energetic.

The reward of a thing well done is to have done it.

ENDEAVOUR

To leave no stone unturned.

ENJOYMENT

Let us eat and drink for tomorrow we shall die.

Restraint is the golden key of enjoyment.

Have a nice day: God made it.

Only mediocrity of enjoyment is allowed to man.

Enjoy when you can and endure when you must.

ENDURING

Put that in your pipe and smoke it.

ENDURANCE

He conquers who endures.

What cannot be cured must be endured.

ENTHUSIASM

No virtue is safe that is not enthusiastic.

The enthusiasm of old men is singularly like that of infancy.

Nothing great was ever achieved without enthusiasm.

If you can give your son only one gift, let it be enthusiasm.

The world belongs to the enthusiast who keeps cool.

I prefer the errors of enthusiasm to the indifference of wisdom.

EQUALITY

Liberty! Equality! Fraternity!

If we don't hang together, we will hang separately.

Let us go hand in hand, not one before the other.

ERROR

To err is human, to forgive divine.

Omissions and commissions excepted.

The cautious seldom err.

ERRING

To err is human.

To err is human; to blame it on the other guy is even more human.

ETERNITY

Eternity is in love with the production of time.

As if you could kill time without injuring eternity.

No man can pass into eternity, for he is already in it.

Evil and good are God's right hand and left.

Time is the image of eternity.

I saw the starry tree eternity, put forth the blossom time.

EVENING

If one lost in the morning returns home in the evening, he should be welcomed.

EVIDENCE

Facts are stubborn things.

EVIL

Evil begets evil.

There is nothing good or bad, but thinking makes it so.

Bad men leave their mark everywhere they go.

Evil often triumphs, but never conquers.

It is a great evil not to be able to bear an evil.

All spirits are enslaved that serve things evil.

Evil alone has oil for every wheel.

EXAMPLE

Children have more need of models than of critics.

Nothing is so infectious as an example.

Example is better than precept.

Example is lesson that all men can read.

Example is better than following it.

EXCELLENCE

Excellent things are rare.

Those whom Gods love die young.

Quality rather than quantity.

EXPECTATION

Everything comes if a man can only wait.

If you have sown thorns do not hope to harvest roses.

Pepper plant will not put forth roses.

Nothing is so good as it seems beforehand.

EXPERIENCE

Experience is the shroud of illusions.

Experience is the best teacher.

A burnt child dreads the fire.

One burnt by milk, blows on buttermilk to cool it.

Experience is the extract of suffering.

Is there anyone so wise as to learn by the experience of others?

We learn to walk by stumbling.

It is the mark of an inexperienced man not to believe in luck.

I was not born yesterday.

I am a part of all that I have met.

Experience is the name everyone gives to his mistakes.

If a man deceives me once, shame on him; if he deceive me twice, shame on me.

EXPERT

An expert is one who knows more and more about less and less.

EYE

Among the blind the one-eyed is king.

The debtor cannot lift his eyes.

An eye for eye, a tooth for tooth.

The eyes believe themselves; the ears believe others.

While buying use your eyes, not your ears.

Eyes are windows of the soul.

A grey eye is a sly eye.

A blue eye is a true eye.

F

FACE

A pretty face is a fortune.

Face tells everything.

The face is the index of the heart (mind).

The worst of faces still is human.

Face is the image of the soul.

A good face is the best letter of recommendation.

Your face is a book, where men may read strange matters.

Trust not too much to an enchanting face.

The man is read in his face.

FACT

Now what I want is, facts, facts alone are wanted in life.

Facts do not cease to exist because they are ignored.

God give me strength to face, a fact though it lay me.

Facts are stubborn things.

Every fact that is learnt becomes a key to other facts.

FAILURE

Every failure is a stepping-stone to success.

He who does not fall, does not rise.

FAIR PLAY

All is fair in love and war.

What is sauce for the goose is sauce for the gander.

Be fair to yourself before you can call others foul.

FAITH

Faith is the continuation of reason.

I can believe anything, provided it is incredible.

If a man has strong faith, he can indulge in the luxury of scepticism.

Faith is the force of life.

Faith is the bird that sings when the dawn is still dark.

The faith that stands on authority is not faith.

FALSE

False in one thing, false in everything.

None but the cowards lie.

Dare to be true; nothing can need in lie.

Round numbers are always false.

Falsehood is a perennial spring.

The ultimate truth is penultimately a falsehood.

FALSE FRIEND

Better an open enemy than a false friend.

FAME

Fame is not popularity.

FAMILIARITY

Familiarity breeds contempt.

Distant friendship is welcome.

All objects lose by too familiar a view.

Be thou familiar, but by no means vulgar.

Few men have been admired by their own servants.

No man is a hero to his valet.

FAMILY

All happy families are alike, but each unhappy family is unhappy in its own way.

None but a mule denies his family.

Family is more sacred than the State.

FAREWELL

Sweet to the sweets

Farewell, May God be with you

We will meet again.

FATHER

A father is a banker provided by nature.

The child is the father of man.

FARMING

Some people tell us that there ain't no hell,
But they never farmed, so how can they tell?

FASHION

Fashion is a form of ugliness.

FATE

God decrees the destiny of men.

The die is cast.

Whatever is to happen will happen.

Only a fool tries to disperse the fog with a fan.

FAULT

Great men have great defects.

There is much good in the worst of us.

One can see a straw in another's eye but not a beam in one's own.

There is some good in the worst of us.

Perfection does not exist in nature.

FEAR

The fear of the Lord is the beginning of knowledge.

Be fearless and have enmity with none.

The only thing we have to fear is fear itself.

FLATTERY

It is easy to flatter, but hard to please.

Imitation is the sincerest form of flattery.

FIRE

Truth cannot be destroyed by fire.

The burnt child dreads the fire.

No smoke without fire.

All the fat's in the fire.

FISH

There are as many good fish in the sea as ever came out of it.

She is neither fish nor flesh nor good red herring.

You must lose a fly to catch a fish.

Angling is an innocent cruelty.

FLY

It is easier to catch flies with honey than with vinegar.

A fly in milk i.e. cause of spoiling joy.

FOOL

A learned fool is more foolish than an ignorant fool.

A fool and his money are soon parted.

Who thinks himself wise is a fool.

FORESIGHT

Look before you leap.

FORGETFULNESS

Out of sight, out of mind.

Good to forgive, best to forget.

Forget and forgive.

FORGIVENESS

To err is human; to forgive, divine.

FORTUNE

Fortune favour fools.

Dilgence is the mother of good fortune.

In fair weather, prepare for foul.

FRANCE

Forty million Frenchmen can't be wrong.

FORTY-FIFTY

Forty is the old age of youth; fifty is the youth of old age.

FOX

A sleeping fox counts hens in his sleep.

FREEDOM

The cause of freedom is the cause of God.

Seek yet first political freedom and all things will be added unto thee.

One hallmark of freedom is the sound of laughter.

The cause of freedom is the cause of God.

Freedom is the oxygen of the soul.

FRIEND

A friend is the one who comes in when the whole world has gone out.

A friend's frown is better than a fool's smile.

A friend to all is a friend to none.

Have but few friends, though many acquaintances.

I cannot be your friend and your flatterer too.

One enemy is too many and a hundred friends too few.

Old friends and old wine are best.

The best mirror is an old friend.

Friends are not made. They're recognised.

A friend is one before whom I may think aloud.

Those who seek faultless friends remain friendless.

Friends are relatives you make for yourself.

Be slow in choosing a friend, slower in changing.

FRUGALITY

A penny saved is penny gained (got).

Penny and penny laid up will be many.

FRIENDSHIP

A friend in need is a friend indeed.

The only way to have a friend is to be a friend.

Reprove your friend in secret, praise him openly.

True friendship is a plant of slow growth.

A backfriend, a shoulder clapper.

Prosperity makes friends, but adversity tries them.

A friend is one who dislikes the same people you dislike.

A true friend is one soul in two bodies.

FRUIT

Stolen fruits are the sweetest.

By their fruits, you shall know them.

Patience yields sweet fruit.

The ripest fruit first falls.

FUTURE

When all is lost, future still remains.

You can know the future from the past.

Whatever will happen, will happen.

The present is great with future.

The greater the power, the more dangerous the abuse.

G

GAMBLING

Man is a gambling animal

Life is a gamble.

GENIUS

Genius is akin to madness.

There must be intelligence even in copying.

GENTLEMAN

Education begins a gentleman, conversation completes him.

It takes three generations to make a gentleman.

To be born a gentleman is an accident; to die one, an achievement.

GENTLENESS

There is nothing stronger in the world than gentleness.

GENERALITIES

He who likes to generalise, generally lies.

GIFT

Never look a gift horse in the mouth.

GIVING

He gives twice who gives quickly.

GOAL

The goal ever recedes from us.

The greater the progress, the greater the recognition of our unworthiness.

Satisfaction lies in the effort, not in the attainment.

Full effort is full victory.

GLORY

Our greatest glory is not in never falling, but in rising everytime we fall.

Desire of glory is the last garment that even wise men put off.

GLUTTONY

If God be for us, who can be against us.

If God did not exist, it would be necessary to invent him.

Gluttony kills more than the sword.

The kingdom of God is within you.

Gluttons dig their graves with their teeth.

GOD

Fear that man who fears not God.

God helps those who help themselves.

Man proposes, God disposes.

Fear of God is the beginning of wisdom.

Be afraid of God in whatever you do.

God sees everything.

GOLDEN RULE

Do not do to others what would anger you, if done to you by others.

Deal with others as thou wouldst thyself by others.

What you want others not to do to you, do not do to others.

Do as you would be done by.

GOOD DEED

A good deed is never lost.

One good deed deserves another.

GOOD

That which is striking and beautiful is not always good, but that which is good is always beautiful.

GOODNESS

Do good, have good.

In all the ways you can, as long as ever you can.

All is good that hath good end.

Handsome is that handsome does,

Return good for evil.

Do all the good you can, To all the people you can,

GOOD SENSE

Bear wealth. Poverty will bear itself.

Better an empty house than an ill tenant.

Better lose a jest than a friend.

Keep your mouth shut and your eyes open.

Of the two evils, choose the least.

Cut your coat according to the cloth.

Do not keep a dog and bark yourself.

He is not laughed that laughs at himself first.
He commands enough that obeys a wise man.
Neither a borrower nor a lender be.
Give every man thy ear, but few thy voice.

GOSSIP

He that repeath a matter separateth many fiends.
While truth travels a mile, a lie covers the globe.

GOOD WIFE

A good wife makes a good husband.
A good wife and health is a man's best friend.

GOODWILL

Good will is earned by many acts; it can be lost by one.

GOOSE

What is sauce for the goose is sauce for the gander.
Do not kill the goose that lays golden eggs.

GOVERNMENT

That which reviews (issues) every minute, is government.
The safety of the State is the highest law.

The king is dead, long live the king!

The government is proverbially said to be a body.

Yes it is a body, but with the vital organs-the head and the heart-missing.

GRATITUDE

Gratitude is the heart's memory.

GREAT THING

The great in this world is not so much where we are, but in what direction we are moving.

GREECE

Beware of Greeks bearing gifts.

GUILT

The lady doth protest too much, me thinks.

We must find ways to starve the terrorist.

GRIEF

Everyone can master a grief, but he that has it.

GRIT

To strive, to seek, to find and not to yield.

GROWING

When we are not sure, we are alive.

The trick is in growing up without growing old.

You're never too old to grow up.

GRUMBLER

One unable to dance blames the unevenness of the floor.

GUEST

Every guest hates the others and the host hates them all.

A guest is for one or two days; on the third day, he is notorious.

A good guest is half his host.

H

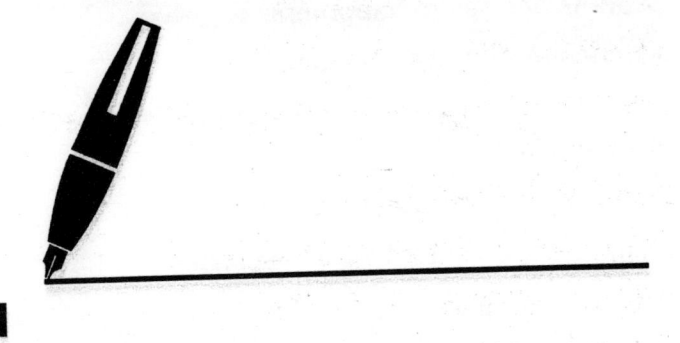

HABIT

Habits are at first cobwebs, then cables.
Custom makes all things easy.
The worst boss anyone can have is a bad habit.
Habit is either the best of servants or the worst of masters.
Habits die hard.

HAIR

Grey hair is a sign of age, not of wisdom.
The very hairs of your head are all numbered.
There was never a saint with red hair.

HAPPINESS

The greatest happiness of the greatest number.
Eat, drink and be merry, for tomorrow we die.

Work is one key to happiness.

Cooperate with the inevitable.

There is no duty we so much under-rate, as the duty of being happy.

Better be born happy than wise.

Happiness is contagious. Be a carrier!

Call no man happy till he dies.

The gift of happiness belongs to those who unwrap it.

The days that make us happy make us wise.

Happiness is belonging, not belongings.

You are genuinely happy if you don't know why.

Happiness makes up in height, for what it lacks in length.

HASTE

Haste makes waste.

Haste is of the Devil.

Make haste slowly.

HATRED

It is hatred that separates man from man; therefore it is wrong and false. It is a disintegrating power, it separates and destroys.

HEAD

Two heads are better than one.

The head is the dupe of the heart.

An old head on young shoulders.

HEAVEN

Earth has no sorrow which heaven cannot heal.

In Heaven an angel is a nobody in particular.

All this and Heaven too!

In my father's house are many mansions.

HEALTH

He who has health has hope and he who has hope has everything.

Health is not a condition of matter but of mind.

Early to bed, early to rise.
Makes a man healthy, wealthy and wise.

An apple a day keeps the doctor away.

After dinner rest a while,
After supper walk a mile.

Keep your feet warm and your head cool,
Then you may call your doctor a fool.

If wealth is lost, nothing is lost.

If health is lost, something is lost.

If character is lost, everything is lost

A sound mind in a healthy body.

HANGING

As well be hanged for a sheep as a lamb.

If we do not hang together, we will hang separately.

HEARING

None so deaf as those who will not hear.

Little pitchers have long ears.

He has both ears to hear, let him hear.

HEART

The heart has its own reasons of which reason knows nothing.

The heart knoweth his own bitterness.

HELL

The road to hell is paved with good intentions.

Hell and heaven are inside us.

Hell is waiting without hope.

Abandon hope, all you enter here.

We are each our own devil and we make this world our hell.

HELPLESSNESS

Beggars cannot be choosers.

But now I am cabin'd, cribb'd, confined.

HELP

God helps those who help themselves.

Light is the task when many share the toil.

Poor man has no friend.

HEREDITY

It runs in the blood like wooden legs.

Breed is stronger than pasture.

The father's have eaten sour grapes and the children's teeth are set on edge.

Such a father, such a son.

Such a mother, such a daughter.

Noble fathers have noble children.

He is a chip of the old block.

Clever father, clever daughter; clever mother, clever son.

HERO

Heroes are made, not born.

No man is a hero to his wife.

No man is a hero to his valet.

No woman is a wife to her own hero.

Heroes are made in the hour of defeat.

Success is, therefore, well described as a series of glorious defeats.

HIGHBROW

A highbrow is a person, who is educated beyond his intelligence.

HINDRANCE

To put a poke in one's wheel.

HINDSIGHT

Ah, the insight of hindsight!

HOPE

Great hopes make great men.

Hope is the staff of life.

The world is established on hope.

Hope for the best, but prepare for the worst.

Hope springs eternal in the human breast.

Hope deferred maketh the heart sick.

Who against hope believes in hope.

Hope is the poor man's bread.

Abandon hope all ye who enter here.

If winter comes, can spring be for behind?

Every cloud has a silver lining.

The darkest hour is before the dawn.

While there is life, there is hope.

For where no hope is left, is left no fear.

When one door shuts, another opens.

Hope is the dream of a waking man.

Even a small star shines in the darkness.

A poor man with hope lives better than a rich man without it.

The tide turns at low water as at high.

HISTORY

What is history, but fable agreed upon?

HOME

An Englishman's home is his castle.

The comfort found in Chajju's attic is not found in luxurious cities of Balk and Bokhara.

There is no place like home.

East or West, home is the best.

Home is where the heart is.

Home, sweet home.

HONESTY

Honesty is the best policy.

After ninety-nine days, the thief is caught on the hundredth.

An honest man's the noblest work of God.

To an honest man, it is an honour to have remembered his duty.

Honest men fear neither the light nor the dark.

HONOUR

Honour lies in honest toil.

Is there no fame in infamy?

The nation's honour is dearer than the nation's comfort.

HORSE

You may lead a horse to water, but you cannot make him drink.

One man may lead a horse to water, but twenty cannot make him drink.

Money makes the mare go.

If wishes were horses, beggars would ride.

A mule that transports for money, i.e. mercenary.

About horses;

One white foot—buy him;
Two white feet—try him;
Three white feet—look about him;
Four white feet-go without him.

A horse! my kingdom for a horse!

HUMANITY

What is human is immortal.

Man is made to worship God

Our true nationality is mankind.

HOSPITALITY

A guest is a guest for two days; on the third he is a pest.

Give your guest what you eat everyday.

Every guest hates the others, and the host hates them all.

HOUSE

Fools build houses and wise men live in them.

He that lives in a glass-house must not throw stones at others.

A foolish man built his house upon the sand.

House is, where the heart is.

HUMILITY

In humility, imitate the earth.

Water runs down, not up.

He that is down, need fear no fall.

Pride goes before a fall.

What I beg from God, is poverty.

After crosses and losses, men grow humbler and wiser.

The higher you go, the lower you will fall.

Death is the great leveller.

Sun rises and sets everyday.

He who rides must not fear a fall.

Humbleness is always grace; always dignity.

Humble thyself in all things.

He who is up, will one day be down.

Humility, like darkness, reveals the heavenly lights.

It is always the secure who are humble.

HUNGER

If thine enemy be hungry, give him bread to eat.

A hungry dog fights best.

When there is no bread in the stomach, everything goes wrong.

O God! I cannot serve you without food. Take away your rosary.

Hunger is worse than death.

What will a hungry man not do?

A hungry stomach is not a good adviser.

Hunger is the best sauce.

HUSBAND

All husbands are alike, but they have different faces, so you can tell them apart.

No life without wife.

A good husband should be deaf and a good wife, blind.

I

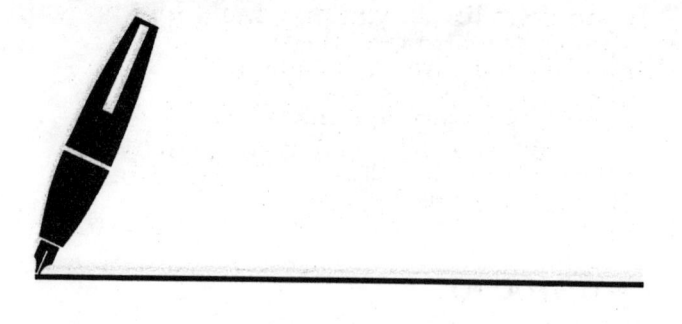

IDEALS

Ideals are like stars; you will not succeed in touching them with your hands. But, like the seafaring man on the desert of waters, you choose them for your guides and following them you will reach your destiny.

IDLENESS

The devil always finds some work for idle hands to do.

An idle man's mind is a devil's workshop.

Better wear out than rust out.

Idleness is the holiday of fools.

To waste your life is as great a sin as to end it.

Idleness is a devil's workshop.

IF

If you run after two hares, you will catch neither.

If you don't like it, you may lump (put up with) it.
If the sky falls, we shall catch larks.
If you make a jest, you must take a jest.
If wishes were horses, beggars would ride.
If you would know the value of money, try to borrow some.
If you want a thing well done, do it yourself.

IGNORANCE

Ignorance is bliss.
Not to know is better than to know something wrong.
Ignorance of law is no excuse.
If knowledge is power, ignorance is a great weakness.
Ignorance is not innocence, but sin.
Ignorance never settles a question.

IMITATION

Imitation is the sincerest flattery.
There can be no good imitation without intelligence.

IMMORTALITY

The soul is immortal.

IMPOSSIBILITY

You can't make a silk purse out of a sow's ear.
You can't get milk out of stone.
All things are difficult before they are easy.
You can't get blood out of turnip.

INGRATITUDE

Don't bite the hand that feeds you.
Ingratitude is a great sin.

INVENTION

Necessity is the mother of invention.
History is invented.

INJUSTICE

Justice delayed is justice denied.
God loves the just.
The sun sees the whole world with one eye.

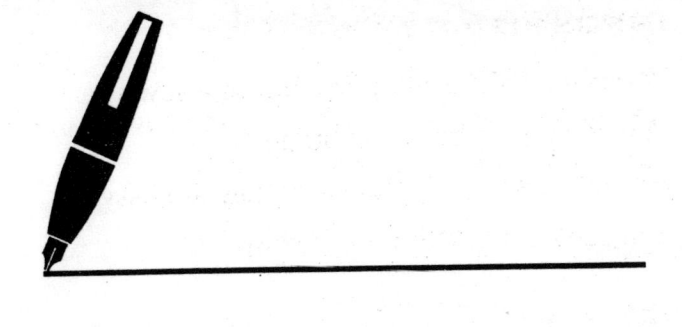

JOKE

Many a true word is spoken in jest.

Jesters do often prove prophets.

A joke is a very serious thing.

My way of joking is to tell the truth. It's the funniest joke in the world.

JUSTICE

The path of justice is as the shining light, that shines more and more unto the perfect day.

There is no justice in or out of courts.

Give the devil his due.

Rigid justice rules the world.

The mills of God grind slowly, but exceeding small.

Let justice be done though the heavens fall.

Justice delayed is justice denied.

Render there to all their dues.

Peace, commerce and honest friendship with all nations; entangling alliances with none.

JOY

Joy is a great medicine.

A laughter is a candle lighted in the house.

JUDGEMENT

It is better that a judge should lean on the side of compassion than severity.

Let the judges answer to the question of law and the jurors to the matter of fact.

Thou art weighed in the balance and found wanting.

Judge not that ye be not judged.

A Daniel come to judgement.

K

KINDNESS

Compassion is the root of religion.

Kindness gives birth to kindness

KISS

Stolen kisses are the sweetest.

Some women blush when they are kissed; some call for the police; some swear; some bite. But, the worst are those who laugh.

KNOWLEDGE

Men are four:

He who knows not and knows not he knows not, he is a fool-shun him;

He who knows not and knows he knows not, he is simple-teach him;

He who knows and knows not he knows, he is asleep-wake him;

He who knows and knows he knows, he is wise-follow him.

Like fire in a piece of flint, knowledge, secular or spiritual, exists in the mind; suggestion is the friction which brings it out.

To be conscious of one's ignorance is a great step to knowledge.

Knowledge is power.

He that increaseth knowledge increaseth sorrow.

One cannot know everything.

He that hath knowledge spareth his words.

Knowledge is higher than power.

To understand is to pardon.

L

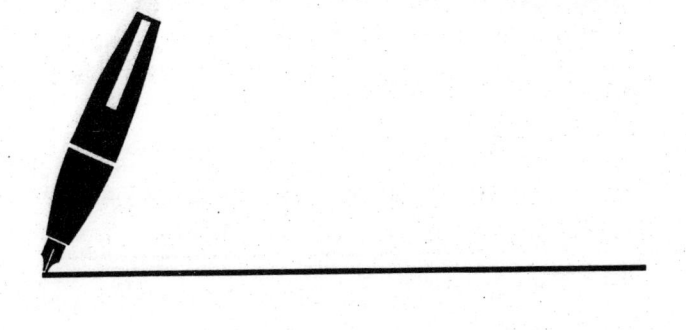

LAUGHTER

He laughs best who laughs last.

Laughter is the best medicine.

Laughter is not at all a beginning of a friendship and it is not the best ending for one.

LAMB

God tempers the wind to the shorn lamb.

LAND

Earth is our mother.

That which is built upon the land goes with the land.

LAW

Possession is nine-tenths of law.

If the laws would speak for themselves, they would complain of the lawyers in the first place.

Law is a bottomless pit.

Might is right.

No laws, however stringent, can make the idle industrious, the thriftless provident, or the drunken sober.

The laws sometimes sleep, but never die.

Petty laws breed great crimes.

The king is above law.

LAWYER

A lawyer's opinion is worth nothing unless paid for.

The hands of a lawyer are in other people's pockets.

LIBERALITY

The liberal soul shall be made fat.

The stream does not feel the loss at all if a sparrow takes a drop out of it.

The more you give, the more you get to give.

Hoarded money becomes foul like standing water.

LEADERSHIP

An army of stags led by a lion would be better than an army of lions led by a stag.

LEARNING

Much learning doth make thee mad.

To be wise is not to be learned.

Learning is a key to progress.

If you throw a handful of jewels into the head of a child, no one will take it away from him.

Cleverness is not wisdom.

LENDING

If you lend, you either lose the money or gain an enemy.

Better give a shilling than lend and lose half a crown.

Neither a lender nor a borrower be.

For loan loses both it and friend.

Nobody's credit is as good as his cash.

LIBERAL

A liberal is one who has both feet firmly planted in the air.

LIBERTY

Liberty's in every blow!

Let's do or die.

Give me liberty or give me death.

Freedom is my birthright.

Liberty! Equality! Fraternity!

Liberty is the mother of all progress.

Too much of liberty is destructive.

LIFE

So little done, so much to do.

Better a living beggar than a buried emperor.

Take life as it comes to you and try to make it as you wish it to be.

Life is a jigsaw puzzle with most of the pieces missing.
Life is a mere bubble.

Life is short, art is long.

For the wise life is a problem; to the fool, a solution.

Life is a walking shadow.

To meet, to know, to live and then to part,
Is the sad tale of many a human heart?

They that mistake life's accessories for life itself are like them that go too fast in a maze, their very haste confuses them.

Life is the art of drawing sufficient conclusions from sufficient premises.

Life is good or bad according to the state of mind in which we look at it; it is neither by itself.

The problem of life is not to make life easier, but to make man stronger.

Life is like playing a violin solo in public and learning the instrument as one goes on.

Life is like a cup of tea, the more heartily we drink the sooner we reach the drops.

Life demands from you only the strength you possess.

Only one feat is possible-not to have run away.

LIKE

Birds of a feather flock together.

One crow will not pick out another crow's eyes.

Like mother, like daughter.

One dog is enemy of another.

Like father, like son.

Such a father, such a son.

He is a chip of the old block.

LIGHT

God said, Let there be light: and there was light.

Below the lamp, there is darkness.

It is darkest before the dawn.

LION

Even a lion has to defend itself against the flies.

Even a dog is lion in its own street.

Lion does not eat a lion.

A lion does not eat a corpse.

Lion do no eat carrots.

LOVE

Love is blind and lovers cannot see.

There's no love lost between us.

Our first love and last love is self-love.

If you would be loved, love and be lovable.

Its's love that makes the world go round.

Life without love is hell.

If no one loves you, go and love someone.

It is easy to hate, but healthy to love.

Love is light.

Love is God.

Love is the key to happiness.

Marry someone who loves you and not someone you love.

Love is the fulfilling of the law.

Blue eyes say, "Love me or I die"; black eyes say, "Love me or I kill thee".

Love makes marriage possible; habit makes it endurable.

Love is more tiring than friendship for it demands continuous prop.

True love is like a ghost which every body talks about but few have seen.

LISTENING

From listening comes wisdom and from speaking repentance.

Walls have ears.

LOGIC

An instrument used for mastering a prejudice.

LUCK

Throw a lucky man into the sea and he will come out with a fish in his mouth.

Good luck is a lazy man's estimate of a worker's success.

Behind bad luck comes good luck.

Pluck is luck.

Luck is pluck.

An ounce of pluck is worth a ton of luck.

Do and dare make destiny.

There's destiny that rules our ends.

Without, luck there is nothing.

We will get, what destiny has allotted to us.

When God gives, He pours through the roof.

LYING

While truth travels a mile, lie goes round the globe.

One lie leads to more lies.

Some circumstantial evidence is very strong, as when you find a trout in the milk.

M

MAMMON

You cannot serve God and Mammon.

MAN

He for God and she for God in him.

Man is made for worship.

Manners make a man.

If you are a man, you are everything.

What a piece of work is man!

Sigh no more, ladies, sigh no more.

Men were deceivers ever.

Man is not the creature of circumstance.

Circumstances are the creatures of men.

It is not the greatness of a man's means that make him independent, so much as the smallness of his wants.

The man who is a pessimist before forty eight knows too much, the man who is an optimist after forty eight knows too little.

A man is as young as he feels, after trying to prove it.

In keeping men off, you keep them on.

The glory, the jest and riddle of the world.

The proper study of mankind is man.

Every man over forty is a scoundrel.

Man is the hunter; woman is his game.

Man is the measure of all things.

No man is born wise.

Lord, what fools these mortals be!

Limited in his nature, infinite in his desire.

Man is a gaming animal.

Man is born free and everywhere he is in chains.

MACHINE

We make machines; machines make us.

Machines cannot live without men, men cannot live without machines.

We have enslaved machines; machines have enslaved us.

Man is a tool-using animal; machine is a man-using tool.

MANNERS

Men make laws; women make manners.

Good manners are the foundation of society.

Manners make the man.

Manners are the happy way of doing things.

Good manners are made up of petty sacrifices.

Civility costs nothing, but buys everything.

Men, like bullets go farthest when they are smoothest.

MAJORITY

Majority has authority.

One with the law is a majority.

MAN AND WOMAN

Men can be analysed, women merely adored.

A man is as old as he feels and a wowan is as old as she looks.

MANAGE

To make ends meet.

MARRIAGE

It is better for a woman to marry a man who loves her, than a man she loves.

Marriage is a romance in which the hero dies in the first chapter.

A deaf husband and a blind wife are always a happy couple.

To marry once is a duty, twice a folly, thrice a madness.

Marriage is popular because it combines the maximum of temptation with the maximum of opportunity.

The strongest man upon earth is he, who stands most alone.

Love is the dawn of marriage and marriage is the sunset of love.

It is not good that man should be alone.

Weeping bride, laughing mother; laughing bride, weeping wife.

Wedding dress:
Something old, something new,
Something borrowed, something blue.

The woman cries before the wedding; the man afterwards.

A prudent wife is from the Lord.

Marriages are made in heaven.

Advise no man to go to marry or to war.

Marriage is that relation between man and woman in which the independence is equal, the dependence mutual and the obligation reciprocal.

MASTER

He that is master of himself will soon be the master of others.

He who pays the piper, may call the tune.

No man can serve two masters.

MEMORY

Human memory is short.

We remember by forgetting.

To remember something worthwhile, we must forget a great many worthless things.

A great memory does not make a philosopher, any more than a dictionary can be called a grammar.

The true art of memory is the art of attention.

Women and elephants never forget.

What we learn through pleasure, we never forget.

Method is the mother of memory.

A good memory is one trained to forget the trivial.

Vanity plays lurid tricks with our memories.

MATURITY

Let not thy will roar, when thy power can but whisper.

You cannot mature until you expect the unexpected.

Maturity is the ability to live in someone else's world.

Maturity is reached the day we don't need to be lied to about anything.

MEDICINE

Physician heals; God cures.

The doctor treats; Nature makes well.

An apple a day keeps the doctor away.

Physician, first heal thyself!

A sound mind in a healthy body.

Bitter pills may have wholesome effects.

The best of all medicines are rest and fasting.

MEDIOCRITY

Jack of all trades, master of none.

He who walks in another's tracks, leaves no footprints.

Only a mediocre person is always at his best.

Mediocrity knows nothing higher than itself.

Mediocrity adds two and two and gets only four.

MERCY

The quality of mercy is not strained.

Compassion is the root of religion.

Do good to those, who do you harm.

Mercy is enthroned in the hearts of kings.

MERRIMENT

A merry heart doth good like medicine.

Eat, drink and be merry.

A merry heart goes all the way; a sad one tires in a mile.

MISER

The miser is always in want.

The miser lacks what he has, as well as what he hasn't.

MIND

Mind is the precursor of all perceptions: mind is the most subtle of all elements in the phenomenal universe.

All objectified consciousness has its origin in the mind.

One who speaks or acts with a pure mind, happiness abides with him as his own shadow.

My mind to me a kingdom is.

Man's mind is like a parachute: to work, first it has to be open.

An empty mind is a devil's workshop.

Few minds wear out; most rust out.

A sound mind in a sound body.

MISERY

Misery loves company.

Poverty multiplies bedfellows.

If winter comes, can spring be far behind?

The miseries of the world cannot be cured by physical help only.

Until man's nature changes, these physical needs will always arise and miseries will always be felt.

MISFORTUNE

Misfortunes always come in by a door, that has been left open for them.

Misfortunes never come alone.

There is fortune even in misfortune.

Everything is for the best in this best of all worlds.

MIXED BLESSING

No rose without a thorn.

MISLEAD

To throw dust in one's eyes.

MISSION

He who has no mission in life, is the poorest of all.

MISTAKE

To have the wrong sow by the ear.

MOB

Mob is a big babe.

The voice of the people, is the voice of God.

The mob has many heads, but no brains.

Nothing is so easy as to train mobs, for the simple reason that they have no mind, no premeditation.

The fickle mob.

MODERATION

Give me neither poverty, nor riches.

To live well, is necessary to live slowly.

Follow the golden mean.

The middle course is the best.

MODESTY

Modesty is the badge of womanhood.

Modesty is the only sure bait when you angled praise.

Modesty died when false modesty was born.

A modest man never talks of himself.

MONARCH

I am the master of all I survey.

MONEY

Money is a good servant, but a bad master.

When a rupee goes out for change, It never returns.

Penny wise, pound foolish.

When I had money, every one called me brother.

Money is honey.

When money speaks truth is silent.

Lack of money is the root of all evil.

Gold is the touchstone whereby to try men.

Even wisdom surrenders to desire of gain.

A wise man should have money in his head, not in his heart.

Ready money is Alladin's lamp.

Money.... is man's personal energy reduced to portable form.

The love of money is the root of all evils.

If money is not thy servant, it will be thy master.

Money talks.

Money begets money.

Money makes the mare go.

No lock will hold against the power of gold.

Money makes the man.

MORTALITY

Man is mortal.

MONTHS

March comes in like a lion and goes out like a lamb.

We are April when we woo, December when we wed

If February gives much snow.
A fine Summer doth it show.
Thirty days hath September,
April, June and November;
All the rest have thrity-one.
Excepting February alone,
Which hath twenty-eight, in fine.
Till leap year gives it twenty-nine.
If cold December gave you birth.
The month of snow and ice and mirth.
Place on your hand a torquoise blue.

Success will bless you whate'er you do.

MOON

The man who comes once in a blue moon.
(Id ka Chaand)

MOTHER

God could not be present everywhere, so He invented mothers.

Earth is the mother of us all.

We are children of Mother Earth.

Mother is the queen of the house.

What is home without the mother?

Mother makes man.

Her children rise up and call her blessed.

MURDER

Murder will out. Thou shalt not kill.

MOUNTAIN

The mountains were in travail to signify the birth of a mouse.

If the mountain won't come to Mohammad, Mohammad must go to the mountain.

MOURN

Blessed are they that mourn; for they shall be comforted.

MOUSE

When a building is about to fall down, all the mice desert it.

When the cat is away, the mice will play.

MUSIC

Music is the food of the soul.

Music is medicine for man.

MYSTERY

There be three things which are too wonderful for me, four which I know not: the ways of an eagle in the air-ways of a serpent upon the rock; the ways of a ship in the midst of the sea and the ways of a man with a maid.

Mystery is the wisdom of blockheads.

Few things are as immutable as the addiction of political groups to the ideas by which they have once won office.

N

NAME

Sticks and stones will break my bones, but names will never hurt me.

A good name is rather to be chosen than great riches.

Name and fame are temporary.

Neither name nor clue will be left behind after death.

Is there no fame in infamy?

NEIGHBOUR

When you buy a house, know your neighbour first.

Thou shalt love thy neighbour as thyself.

When your neighbour's house is at fire, your own property is at stake.

No one is rich enough to do without a neighbour.

NATURE

Nature is the universal mother.

Nature cures us all.

Doctor treats; Nature cures.

Nature abhors a vacuum.

Cold natures have only recollections; tender natures have remembrances.

One touch of nature makes the whole world kin.

Nature, red in tooth and claw.

Nature is not governed except by obeying her.

Nature is the art of God.

NECESSITY

Necessity is the mother of invention.

Necessity is the best adviser.

Necessity is often the spur to genius.

Necessity makes even the timid brave.

Necessity knows no law.

NEMESIS

Whoso diggeth a pit shall fall therein.

The wheel is come full circle.

Thus the whirligig of time brings in his revenges.

NEUTARLITY

The heart is never neutral.

NOTHINGNESS

They laboriously know nothing.

There is an income tax, the just will pay more and the unjust less.

NEWNESS

There is no new thing under the sun.

NEWS

If a man bites a dog, that is news.

As cold water to thirsty soul, so is good news from a far country.

NEWSPAPER

A good newspaper is a nation talking to itself.

Newspapers are the world's mirrors.

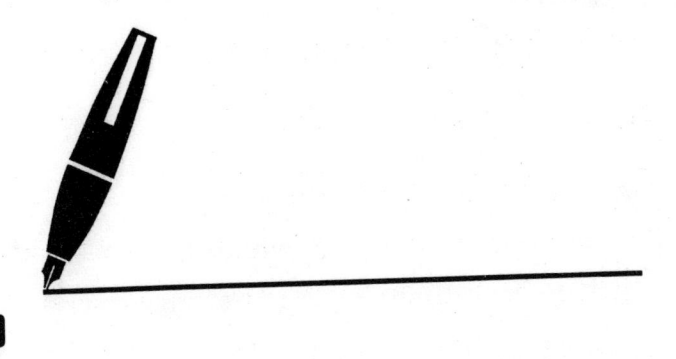

OBEDIENCE

Obedience alone gives the right to command.

The eye that mocketh at his father and despiseth to obey his mother, the ravens of the valley shall pack it out and the young eagles shall eat it.

OCEAN

Praise the sea, but keep to the land.

The ocean has as good fishes as ever came out of it.

Little boats should sail near the shore.

OPTIMISM

Optimism is a cheerful frame of mind that enables a teakettle to sing though in hot water up to its nose.

OPINION

Stiff in opinion, always in the wrong.

OPPORTUNITY

Make hay while the sun shines.

Do not let grass grow under your feet.

Catch an opportunity by the forelock.

Plough deep while sluggards sleep.

OYSTER

The world's an oyster which you can open with the sword.

Put your heart, mind, intellect and soul even to your smallest acts. This is the secret of success.

An optimist sees an opportunity in every calamity; a pessimist sees a calamity in every opportunity.

ORATORY

Honeyed words sweeten the heart.

ORDER

Have a place for everything and everything in its place.

Set thine house in order.

Let all things be done decently and in order.

P

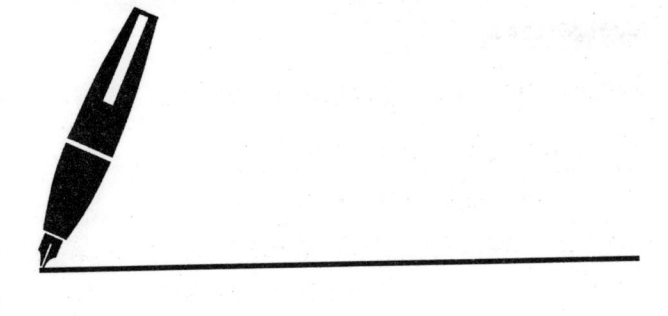

PAIN

Man endures pain as an undeserved punishment; woman endures it as a natural heritage.

There is no gain without pain.

Pain is the beginning and end of life.

The pain of the mind is worse than the pain of the body.

PAINTING

Pictures must not be too picturesque.

A picture is a poem without words.

PARADISE

There is no greater paradise than peace of mind.

Look for the paradise inside, not outside.

If paradise is on earth, it is this, it is this, it is this.

PARENTS

Next to God thy parents.

Such a father, such a son.

Like mother; like daughter.

Clever father, clever daughter; clever mother, clever son.

The first half of our lives is ruined by our parents and the second half by our children.

PARTING

To meet, to know, to live and then to part.
Is the sad tale of many a human heart.

PARTY

Parties help to keep each other in check.

He serves best, who loves his country most.

Party honesty is party expediency.

Parties try to eat each other like snakes.

PASSION

Passion is universal humanity.

Passion is madness.

Knowledge of mankind is a knowledge of their passions.

Passion conquers reason.

PAST

Let bygones be bygones.

What is the use of regretting when sparrows have eaten up the crop?

There is no use of crying over spilt milk.

Past is great with future.

Comes morning, comes dawn, thus our life ends.

Those who cannot remember the past are condemned to relive it.

We sleep by night, eat by day and give away the pearl of our life for the sea-shell.

The past is a bucket of ashes.

The best prophet of the future is the past.

PATIENCE

Patience is the art of hoping.

Patience conquers everything.

A handful of patience is worth more than a bushel of brains.

All things come to him, who can wait.

Patience is bitter, but its fruit is sweet.

The secret of nature is patience.

Learn to labour and to wait.

He who has patience, can have everything.

Patience conquers mountains.

How poor are they who have no patience.

Beware the fury of a patient man.

One is a master, only when one brings to things the patience, to which they are entitled.

PATRIOTISM

My country, right or wrong.

Love of country is the root of great achievements.

No man can be a patriot on an empty stomach.

Patriotism is not enough.

Patriotism is the last refuge of a scoundrel.

The world is my country.

I am a citizen of the world.

PEACE

Peace cannot be achieved through passive neutralism, which would mean withdrawal from the battle for peace.

There can be no peace in the world unless there is peace in the heart.

The most unfair peace is better than the most righteous war.

When reason rules the mind, peace rules the day.

Nation shall not lift up sword against nation.

Unless there is peace inside, there can be no peace outside.

The wolf shall dwell with the lamb and the leopard shall lie down with the kid.

Peace hath her victories no less renowned than war.

Her ways are ways of pleasantness and all her paths are peace.

Mercy and truth have met together: righteousness and peace have kissed each other.

If you want peace, get ready for war.

PEN

The pen is mightier than the sword.

PHILANTHROPY

Steal the hog and give the feet for alms.

I was eye to the blind and feet was I to the lame.

Let not thy left hand know what the right hand doeth.

PEOPLE

The voice of the people is the voice of God.

Vox populi vox Dei.

(Janta ki awaz Parmatma ki awaz hai).

(Panchou main parmesher).

There is God in five men together.

PERSEVERANCE

The waters wear the stone.

Constant dripping wears the stone.

Patience moves mountains.

Victory belongs to the most persevering.

PESSIMISM

A pessimist is one who feels bad when he feels good, lest he feels worse when he feels better.

PHILOSOPHY

Leisure is the mother of philosophy.

PITY

Compassion is the root of religion.

A man without pity is a man without ditty.

Do as you would be done by.

Pity is a natural religion of humanity.

He that hath pity lendeth unto the Lord and that which he hath given will He repay him again.

To be petty is to be without pity.

PLAGIARISM

Shakespeare breathed upon dead bodies and brought them to life.

Don't lard your lean books with the fat of other's works.

The plagiarist pilfers the honey ready for the hive.

We are all wholesale borrowers.

POET

Poets are born, not made.

Nobody can be a poet without madness in him.

All men are poets at heart.

It needs a poet to understand a poet.

The man is either mad or making verses.

Every man is a poet when he is in love.

PLEASURE

Men of leisure are men of pleasure.

Joy is a toy.

Before you make pleasure a business, make business a pleasure.

There is no pleasure without a tinge of bitterness.

Pleasure is followed by pain.

Pleasure follows pain as pain follows pleasure.

Be free from the pairs of opposites, pleasure and pain.

If you want to get rid of pain, get ride of pleasure.

Pleasure today means pain tomorrow.

He that hath loved pleasure shall be a poor man.

POETRY

Let your poem be kept unpublished for nine years.

Poetry is truth dwelling in beauty.

POISON

One man's meat is another's poison.

What is honey for one is poison for another.

POLICY

Honesty is the best policy.

It is easier to catch flies with honey than with vinegar.

POLITICS

Politics is a devil's game.

Politics is the last resort of a scoundrel.

A politician is an animal who can sit on a fence and yet keep both ears close to the ground.

A politician thinks of the next election; a statesman thinks of the next generation.

Majority has authority.

Nothing is politically right what is morally wrong.

Something is rotten in the state of Denmark.

Politics is the art of human happiness.

POPULARITY

Popularity is a mere breath of the people.

If you think well of the people, you are bound to be unpopular.

POSSESSION

Possession is nine-tenths of the law.

When we own a house, the house owns us.

Unto every one that hath shall be given and he shall have abundance, but from him that hath not shall be taken away even that which he hath.

POST

Neither snow, nor rain, nor heat, nor night stays these couriers from the swift completion of their appointed.

POTTERY

Hath not the potter power over the clay of the same lump to make one vessel unto honour and another unto dishonour?

POSTERITY

Such a father, such a son.

Past is an index of future.

Breed is stronger than pasture.

Humanity is one brotherhood.

POVERTY

Out of nothing, nothing comes.

What I beg from God is poverty.

Only the poor can pay.

The rich are needy themselves.

Only the poor can be generous.

Idleness breeds poverty.

The poor have no friends.

The poor shall be always with us.

He that hath pity upon the poor lendeth unto the Lord.

Blessed are the poor.

Poverty is no sin.

To be poor in matter is to be rich in mind.

Those who suffer here, will enjoy hereafter.

The poor are the salt of the earth.

Poverty is the parent of revolution and crime.

Poverty may partly eclipse a man, but it cannot totally obscure him for all time.

POWER

Might is right.

All power belongs to the people.

The buffalo belongs to the one with the rod.

Power always corrupts.

Absolute power corrupts absolutely.

Power is stronger than wine or woman.

The powerful has no pity.

Lust of power is the most flagrant of all passions.

All power is not to all.

PRAISE

Praise the wise man behind his back, but a woman to her face.

The sweetest of all sounds is praise.

Praise the seas but on shore remain.

PREACHING

Practice yourself what you preach.

Do as we say, not as we do.

Preaching is the worst of all trades, but the best of all professions.

He preaches well who lives well.

PRAYER

Prayer is the voice of faith.

Every one that asketh receiveth and he that seeketh, findeth.

Knock and it shall be opened unto thee.

Whatever a man prays for, he prays for a miracle.

Every prayer reduces itself to him: "Great god, grant that twice two be not four.

PREJUDICE

He hears but half who hears one party only.

Prejudice is the child of ignorance.

PREPAREDNESS

We should lay up in peace, what we shall need in war.

PRISONS

Altruism, duty, family, country humanity are the prisons of the soul when they are not its instruments.

PRIDE

Pride goes before a fall.

The proud will be humbled.

The head of pride will hang down.

He who rises in glory, sinks in pride.

PROGRESS

When we go forward in one direction, we go backward in the other.

If we are not going forward, we are going backward.

All progress is imaginary.

We are struggling up the struggling wave.

All that is has been.

There is nothing new under the sun.

Progress is to be measured by the amount of suffering undergone by the sufferer.

The purer the suffering, the greater the progress.

PROMISE

A promise-breaker is a shoemaker.

PROPHECY

We know in part and guess by art.

A prophet is not without honour, save in his own country and in his own house.

Past is the best prophet of the future.

PROOF

The proof of the pudding is in the eating.

You may prove anything by figures.

History is a box of letters.

The burden of proof lies on the plaintiff.

Prove all things; hold fast to that which is good.

PROPERTY

Mine is better than ours.

We belong to the property as much as the property belongs to us.

It is not lawful for me to do, what I will with mine own.

PROSPERITY

The desert shall rejoice and blossom as a rose.

Length of days is in her right hand and in her left hand riches and honour.

Nobody ever became rich by labour alone.

PROVIDENCE

God provides even for a worm in the black stone.

PRUDENCE

Trust in God and keep the powder dry.

A fox counts hen in her sleep.

People who live in glass houses must not throw stones others.

He that fights and runs away, will live to fight another day.

PUBLIC

The public is a big baby.

The majority has authority.

PUNCTUALITY

Time is money.

Napoleon lost war because he was late by five minutes.

Sometimes seconds cost centuries.

Time is costly, Life is more costly.

PUNISHMENT

Eye for eye, tooth for tooth, hand for hand, foot for foot.

Who sheddeth man's blood, by man his blood shall be shed.

No one should be twice punished for one crime.

It was better for him that a millstone was hung about his neck and he cast into the sea.

He that spareth his rod hateth his son.

It is more dangerous to weep inside your mind than to weep in the open.

The open tears can be easily wiped away, but secret tears create scars.

Q

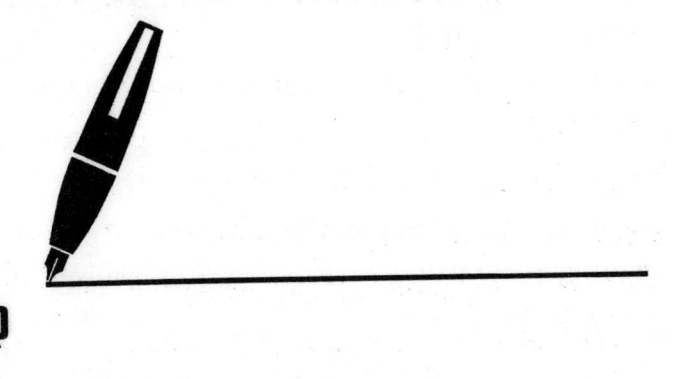

QUARRELLING

The test of a man's or a woman's breeding is how he or she behaves in a quarrel.

It takes two to quarrel.

You cannot clap with one hand.

In quarrelling, the truth is lost.

The quarrels of lovers are the renewal of love.

Fall not out with a friend for a trifle.

People generally quarrel because they cannot argue.

Quarrels would not last long if the wrong were only on one side.

QUESTIONS

It is not every question that deserves an answer.

Ask me no questions and I will tell you no lies.

One of the secrets of life is to make stepping-stones out of stumbling blocks.

QUALITY

Quality is more important than quantity.

Many are called but few are chosen.

There is little choice in rotten apples.

It is not how long, but how well we live.

You may know by a handful the whole sack.

The true worth of a man is to be measured by the objects he pursues.

The best is the cheapest.

R

RACE

God hath made of one blood all nations of men.

Breed is stronger than pasture.

RAIN

After rains cometh fair weather.

Every cloud has a silver lining.

It never rains, but it pours.

RASCALS

Rascals are always sociable and the chief sign that a man has any nobility in his character, is the little pleasure he takes in other's company.

RAINBOW

No happiness without pain, no rainbow without rain.

A rainbow in the morning.
Is the Shepherd's warning.
But a rainbow at night.
Is the Shepherd's delight.

READING

Reading maketh a full man.

Reading is not feeding.

The more you read, the less you understand.

Learn to live, not live to learn.

Read, mark, learn and inwardly digest.

Reading is to the mind what exercise is to the body.

Reading without reflecting is like eating without digesting.

The art of reading is to skip judiciously.

Some people read only because they are too lazy to think.

Always read and think aloud.

Reading serves for delight, for ornament, for ability.

RELATIVES

The worst hatred is that of relatives.

Friendship is dearer than family.

No man will be respected by others, who is despised at home.

The prophet is not honoured at home.

REASON

Reason is the queen of all things.

Come now and let us reason together.

Every why hath a wherefore.

REFORM

Reforms should begin at home and stay there.

Reform! first reform yourself.

Inform the mind before you reform the man.

RELIGION

One religion is as another.

Compassion is the root of religion.

Religion is the opium of the people.

RESPONSIBILITY

Responsibility is not to be shirked, but to be faced boldly.

REPUBLIC

Republics are ungrateful.

RESIGNATION

The Lord gave and the Lord hath taken away; blessed be the name of the Lord.

Job feels the rod, Yet bless God.

You must submit to God against whom you can do nothing.

RESULT

By their fruits, you shall know them.

Whoso diggeth a pit shall fall therein.

RESURRECTION

Earth to earth, ashes to ashes, dust to dust, in sure and certain hope of resurrection.

RETRIBUTION

The mills of God grind slowly, but they grind exceedingly small.

The way of transgressors is hard.

REVENGE

Vengeance is a dish that should be eaten cold.

REVOLUTION

Revolutions are not about trifles, but spring from trifles.

Revolutions are born, not made.

Long live the revolution!

RICHES

If wealth is lost, nothing is lost;

If health is lost, something is lost;
If character is lost, everything is lost.

Early to bed, early to rise
Makes a man healthy, wealthy and wise.

A little house well-filled,

A little land well-tilled,
And a little wife well-willed
Are great riches.

Lay not up for yourself treasures upon earth, where moth and rust doth corrupt and where thieves break through and steal.

A man's true wealth is the good he does in the world.

RIDICULE

Do not make a joke.

If you cannot take a joke.

He will laugh thee to scorn.

RIGHT

Two wrongs can never make a right.

Might is right.

Majority is always in the right.

He who has the rod has the buffalo.

RIGHT THING

Remember there's always a voice saying the right thing to you somewhere if you all only listen to it.

ROME

Rome was not built in a day.

While in Rome, do as Romans do.

See Rome before you die.

ROYALTY

The king reigns, but does not rule.

There is no royal road to success.

The king is dead, long live the king.

Kings have ears but no eyes.

Uneasy lies the head that wears a crown.

Kings are always ungrateful.

Kings have followers but no friends.

Royal affairs are as unpredictable as the track of the river in floods.

RUMOUR

While truth walks a mile, rumour travels round the whole world.

What some invent, others enlarge.

Fibs fly fast.

Truth trudges, falsehood flies.

He who tells all he knows, also tells what he does not.

Keep on reviewing your basics.

S

SAFETY

One is greatest in danger when one thinks himself to be the safest.

It is better to be safe than sorry.

A bird in hand is worth two in the bush.

The trodden path is the safest.

Who will watch the watchers?

Let sleeping dogs lie.

Barking dogs seldom bite.

A wise enemy is better than a foolish friend.

There is no safety against death.

Prevention is better than cure.

SAILOR

Those who sail often, are drowned at last.

One at sea may die in bed.

SCIENCE

Art is I, Science is we.

Science is nothing put perception.

Science is organised knowledge.

Science is simply commonsense at its best.

SCRIPTURE

Even a devil can quote the Bible for his purpose.

SCULPTURE

Sculpture is God's grandchild.

Statues do not sweep.

SEA

Praise the sea; on shore remain.

Ocean knows not its secrets.

A drowning man catches at a straw.

A tiny leak sinks a ship.

The sea hath no king, but God alone.

All rivers flow into the sea.

Do not put an ocean in a nutshell.

SEASON

Spring is a virgin,
Summer a mother,
Autumn a widow,
And winter a stepmother.

Birds of a feather flock together.

A single swallow does not make summer.

Birds sing in the spring.

We are April when we woo, December when we wed.

It never rains, but pours.

SECRECY

There is a skeleton in every house.

Murder will out.

Secret things belong only to God.

If you wish another to keep a secret, first keep it yourself.

No woman can keep a secret.

Walls have ears.

SELFISHNESS

The greedy are needy.

Only the poor can give.

Charity begins at home.

Selfishness is the only real atheism.

Self-love is first and last love.

Every bird feathers its own nest.

SELF-KNOWLEDGE

First know thyself.

All knowledge begins with the self.

Self-knowledge is the foundation of all knowledge.

We know what we are, but know not what we may be.

SELF-MADE

Every man is the architect of his own fortune.

Man is the maker of his own misfortune.

What man has made of man!

He is a self-made man who worships his creature.

He that is down need fear no fall.

SELF-PRAISE

There is no better sauce than self-praise.

God hates those who praise themselves.

Self-praise is no recommendation.

Let another man praise thee and not thine own mouth.

SHADOW

Coming events cast their shadows before.

What shadows we are, what shadows we pursue.

Man is a shadow of shadows.

SELF-RELIANCE

God helps those who help themselves.

An ounce of pluck is worth a ton of luck.

A man is a lion in his own cause.

Doubt whom you will, but never yourself.

SERVICE

Service bears fruit.

They also serve, who only stand and wait.

He profits most, who serves best.

My heart is ever at your service.

First serve, then deserve.

Those who obey best, command best.

SHAME

One who is lost to shame, is lost.

Shame is an ornament for the young.

SHEEP

A leap year.

Is never a good sheep year.

The black sheep do not weep.

There is a black sheep in every herd.

Beware of the black sheep.

Black sheep can grow white wool.

SHIP

They go down to the see in ships, that do business in great waters.

Ships are but boards, sailors but men.

Great ships do not sail in shallow waters.

SHOE

He who wears the shoe, knows where it pinches.

They that make shoes go barefoot themselves.

Shoemaker, stick to your last.

SICKNESS

Be not slow to visit the sick.

In sickness, enemies become brothers.

A friend in need is a friend indeed.

Disease deals dearly.

Prevention is better than cure.

What cannot be cured, must be endured.

Desperate maladies require desperate remedies.

A sound mind in a sound body.

Sickness is a luxury.

SIMPLICITY

To be simple is to be great.

Simplicity is the art of artlessness.

Affected simplicity is refined imposture.

A man is simple, when he is honestly human.

The sublimest are the simplest.

Be simple, not simpleton, childlike, not childish.

SILENCE

Be silent and safe; silence never betrays you.

Speech is silver; silence is golden.

Silence is consent.

Silence is more eloquent than words.

Better be silent than talk bosh.

Still waters run deep.

Empty vessels make much noise.

Barking dogs seldom bite.

Silence is the unbearable repartee.

Keep quiet and people will think you are a philosopher.

The rest is silence.

But silence is most noble till the end.

Silence is better than unmeaning words.

Silence is a very small virtue, but to speak what should not be uttered is a heinous crime.

SIN

Sinner is winner.

Sin has many tools, but a lie is the handle, which fits them all.

I do not seek redemption from the consequences of my sin. I seek to be redeemed from sin itself or rather from the very thought of sin, till I have attained that end I shall be content to be restless.

He that is without sin, let him cast the first stone.

So many laws argue so many sins.

There is no saint, who is also not a sinner.

There is no vice without virtue.

The wages of sin is death.

I am more sinned against than sinning.

Secret guilt by silence is betrayed.

SLAVERY

Corrupted free men are the worst slaves.

They are slaves who fear to speak for the fallen and the weak.

They are slaves who dare not be in the right with two or three.

If you put one end of a chain round a slave's neck, the other end clings to your own throat.

SINCERITY

There can be no true friendship without sincerity.

SCEPTICISM

The sceptics are never deceived.

Believe nothing and be on your guard against everything.

Great intellects are sceptical.

He who disbelieves everybody cannot believe himself.

SKY

The sky is the limit.

The sky is everywhere.

SLANDER

Do not speak ill of a friend behind his back.

Do not cut your nose to spite your face.

Do not wash dirty linen in public.

SLEEP

Sleep is the best cure for sleeping troubles.

The sleep of a labouring man is sweet.

After supper rest a while.

Early to bed, early to rise,
Makes a man healthy, wealthy and wise.

One hour's sleep before midnight is worth three after.

SMILE

Smiles form the channels of a future tear.

He who laughs last, laughs best

Laughter is the best medicine.

The cheerful goes a mile; the cheerless tires in a while.

SONG

Music is the food of the soul.

Our sweetest songs are those that tell of saddest thought.

SNOW

Year of snow, Fruit will grow.

SOCIETY

A man is known by the company he keeps.

Birds of a feather, flock together.

Man is a social animal.

SOLDIER

The king of France with twenty thousand men went up the hill and then came down again; The king of Spain with twenty thousand more, climbed the same hill, the French had climbed before.

God and a soldier all people adore in time of war, but not before; And when war is over and all things are righted, God is neglected and an old soldier slighted.

SOLITUDE

We are never less alone than when alone.

Solitude is the mother of creation.

Solitude is dangerous to reason, without being favourable to virtue.

Remember that the solitary mortal is certainly luxurious, probably superstitious and possibly mad.

SORROW

The sorrow bade good-morrow.

Care will kill a cat.

The busy have no time for tears.

All sorrows are bearable, if there is bread.

The deeper the sorrow, the less tongue hath it.

Every cloud has a silver lining.

There can be no rainbow without a cloud.

SOUL

As you feed the body, do not forget to feed the soul.

Music is the food of the soul.

A sound mind in a sound body.

Every man is the captain of his soul.

What is a man profited, if he shall gain the whole world and lose his own soul?

SOUND

An empty vessel makes much noise.

SPEECH

Brevity is the soul of wit.

Hear much; speak little.

Speech is silver, silence is golden.

Let your speech be always with grace, seasoned with salt.

Miss not the discourse of the elders.

Out of the abundance of the heart, the mouth speaketh.

Rhetoric is the art of ruling the minds of men.

Do not speak ill of the absent.

A soft answer turneth away wrath.
Speak after the manner of men.
Speech is the index of the mind.
The voice of the people is the voice of God.
A bird is known by its note, a man by his talk.

STUDY

Much study is a weariness of the flesh.
Iron sharpens iron; scholar, the scholar.

STYLE

Style is the dress of thought.
Clearness ornaments profound thoughts.
Style is man.

STAR

Hitch your wagon to the star.
Stars are blessed candles of the night.

STATE

People get the government, they deserve.
States are as the men are.
Ambassadors are eyes and ears of a state.
States as great engines, move slowly.

STATEMANSHIP

A politician thinks of the next election; a statesman thinks of the next generation.

STIGMA

Any stigma will do to beat a dogma.

STORM

Ride the whirlwind and reap the storm.

STRANGER

A stranger's eyes see clearest.

I was a stranger and you took me in.

Gold is a stranger in the house of God.

Wealth and weal are strange bedfellows.

STRENGTH

Union is strength.

We must hang together or hang separately.

One is one and two, eleven.

Strength is made perfect in weakness.

As thy days, so shall thy strength be.

Three things give hardy strength; sleeping on hairy mattresses, breathing cold air and eating dry food.

It is excellent to have a giant's strength, but tyrannous to use it like a giant.

Strength comes from an indomitable will.

SUCCESS

Success depends also upon knowing how long would take to succeed.

Nothing succeeds like successful minds work like gimlet to a single point.

Success is counted sweetest by those who never succeed, is not the swift, nor battle to the strong.

Those who climb the highest, fall the lowest.

Since we are in it, we must win it.

The fool tries to win success, the wise to deserve it.

Opposition may be a big incentive to success.

SUFFERING

Suffering is the lot of man.

Since Adam's fall.
We have sinned all.

When bitter becomes bitterest, it becomes a bit rest.

Suffering is the badge of humanity.

There is no success without suffering.

Troubles come not in single files, but in battalions.

It requires more courage to suffer than to die.

SWAN

All geese are not swans.

SWEETNESS

Every sweet hath its sour.

Sweet meat must have sour sauce.

SUICIDE

It is cowardice to commit suicide.

It is easier to end life than to mend it.

SUMMER

We are April when we woo, December when we wed.

Maids are May before they are married.

One swallow does not make summer.

If winter comes, can spring be far behind?

SUN

Make hay while the sun shines.

The sun sees the whole world with one eye.

The sun shines even on the wicked.

SUPERSTITION

Superstition is the religion of feeble minds.

Religion is not removed by removing superstition.

SUSPICION

Little minds nurse great suspicions.

There is a straw in the beard of a guilty person.

Suspicions always haunt the guilty mind.

The thief doth fear each bush an officer.

The less we know, the more we suspect.

SYMPATHY

Sweet words turn away wrath.

He prayeth best, who loveth best.

Justice should not only be done, but should manifestly and undoubtedly be seen to be done.

T

TALE

Beware of him that telleth tales.

A tale never loses in the telling.

TALENT

Concealed talent brings no reputation.

True talent is taking pains.

TALK

Talk is cheap.

Much boast, little roast.

Good talkers are no good doers.

He who talks too much, commits a sin.

TASTE

Every one to his taste.

Good taste is the flower of good sense.

TAX

Render unto Caesar what is Caesar's.

Death and taxes are inevitable.

THIEVING

Thou shall not steal.

Honesty is the best policy.

A thief is a businessman's step-brother.

There is honour among thieves.

Stolen goods run quicker than the thief!

Set a thief to catch a thief.

The lock-breaker is a nephew of the lock-maker.

The thief is a kinsman of the constable.

When thieves fall out, honest men come to their own.

Stolen fruits are the sweetest.

Stolen waters are sweet.

A plague on it when thieves cannot be true one to another!

TEACHING

To tell, is not always to teach.

Each one, teach one.

You cannot teach old dogs, new tricks.

Speak to the earth and it shall teach thee.

TEARS

Tears are Summer showers to the soul.

Tears shall be weeping and gnashing of teeth.

Tears are the silent language of grief.

TEMPERANCE

Drinking water neither makes a man sick, nor in debt, nor his wife a widow.

TEMPTATION

Blessed is the man that endureth temptation.

Get thee behind me, Satan! Lead me not into temptation.

TEST

One of the tests of leadership is the ability to recognise a problem, before it becomes an emergency.

THEOLOGY

Let us put theology out of religion.

Theology has always sent the worst to heaven, the best to hell.

THANKFULNESS

Beggar that I am, I am even poor in thanks.

Even a beggar is not poor in thanks.

Give me some francs, not thanks.

Play your best part with a thankful heart.

THOUGHT

Mind moves mountains.

Faith works miracles.

The power of thought is the magic of the mind.

Second thoughts are best.

Learning without thought is labour lost.

A penny for your thought.

As he thinketh in his heart, so he is.

There is nothing good or bad, but thinking makes it so.

Great thoughts come from the heart.

The more a man thinks, the better adapted he becomes in thinking and education, is nothing if it is not the methodical creation of the habit of thinking.

THRIFT

Penny wise, pound foolish.

A penny saved is a penny earned.

It is better to have a hen tomorrow, than an egg today.

He that will not stoop for a pin, will never be worth a pound.

TODAY

Only the fools water last year's crop.

We are here today and gone tomorrow.

One today is worth two tomorrows.

Do not put off till tomorrow what you can do today.

Fools look back and repent, wise men learn from past follies and act.

TIME

Time and tide wait for nobody.

Time is money.

Haste makes waste.

Do not save minutes and waste lives.

In time, take time while time doth last,

For time is no time when time is past.

A stitch in time saves nine.

My days are swifter than a weaver's shuttle.

Time tests truth.

Time heals all wounds.

Better wear out than rust out.

Man of leisure, is a man of pleasure.

An age builds up cities; an hour destroys them.

There is a time for all things.

There is a season for everything to grow, ripe and fall.

Retime by the forelock.

Do not put off till tomorrow, what you can do today.

Even this will pass away.

It is carved in granite - fools lose time, wise men find it.

Time is the stuff that life is made of, than squander not.

Time if thou dost love life.

TOLERANCE

Live and let live.

Tolerance is the best religion.

Tolerance tests truth.

TREE

Tall oaks from little acorns grow.

A tree is known by the fruit it bears.

Roses have thorns.

Pepper plant will not give birth to roses.

Nip the evil in the bud.

TONGUE

Be clean in thought, word and deed.

Tongue is sharper than a sword.

Speech is silver, silence is golden.

Think before you speak.

It is the spoken word, that rules the world.

TRAVELLING

Travel teaches tolerance.

The longest way round is the shortest way home.

Those who go far, they fare worse.

Travel is the best part of education.

What those know of England, who only England know?

I like to visit New York, but I won't live there if you gave it to me.

East or West, home is best.

East and West you may roam,

There is no place like home.

See Naples before you die.

Delhi is yet far off!

If you forget the way in the morning and return home in the evening, you have not lost much.

The enjoyment you get in a poor Chajju's hut, you will not find in distant cities like Bulagh and Bokhara.

Better buy an air-conditioner, than go to the hills.

TYRANNY

Bad laws are the worst form of tyranny.

Resistance to tyrants, is obedience to God.

This time to fear when tyrants seem to kiss.

It is impossible to find God outside of ourselves.

We are the greatest temple.

TROUBLE

Never trouble till trouble troubles you.

He that seeks trouble always finds it.

Troubles never come in single files, but in battalions.

Man is born into troubles.

TRUST

Trust in God and keep the powder dry.

Trust breeds trust.

TRUTH

Truth will triumph.

Time tests truth.

While truth walks a mile, gossip goes round the globe.

Truth is stranger than fiction.

Error is mortal; truth is immortal.

The truth, the whole truth and nothing but the truth.

It takes two to speak the truth.

U

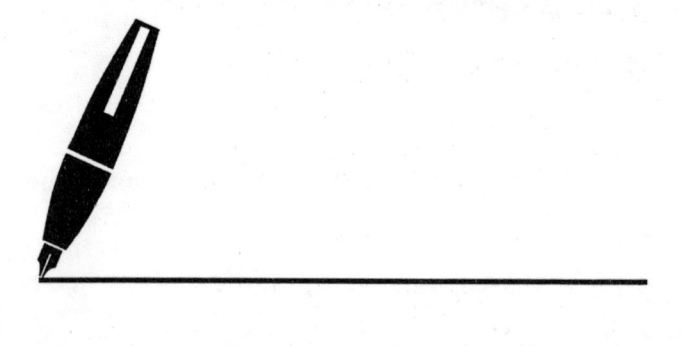

UGLINESS

Handsome is that handsome does.

Better an ugly face than an ugly mind.

UNION

Union is strength.

One for all, all for one.

Hang together or hang separately.

United we stand, divided we fall.

One is one, two are eleven.

Small threads make a strong cord to tie an elephant.

The universe is not hostile, nor yet is it friendly. It is simply indifferent.

Whatever happens at all happens as it should; thou will find this true, if thou shouldst watch narrowly.

UNBUSINESSLIKE ACTION

To carry coals to Newcastle.

UNDERSTANDING

To understand all, is to forgive all.

UNEXPECTED

The unexpected always happens.

UNIQUENESS

Nature made him and then broke the mould.

UNITY

All for one, one for all.

UNIVERSALITY

He was not of an age, but for all time.

UNWISE LOVER

One that loved not wisely, but too well.

The most valuable of all talents is that of never two words when one will do.

UNPROFITABLE

The game is not worth the candle.

UNREVERSIBLE

Things done, cannot be undone.

Things past cannot be recalled.

V

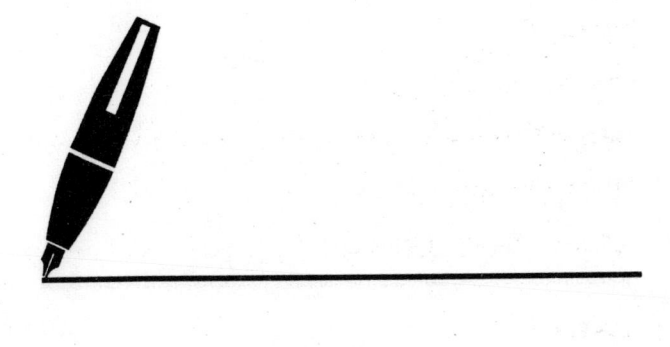

VALOUR

Discretion is the best part of valour.

Valour is of no service, chance rules all and the bravest often fall at the hands of cowards.

The brave alone deserve the fair.

Cowards die many times; the brave die, but once.

Be brave, not slave.

Dare to do your duty always; this is the height of true valour.

VARIETY

Variety is the spice of life.

It takes all sorts to make a world.

So many men, so many opinions.

Variety is the soul of pleasure.

VALUE

Easy come, easy go.

Keep a thing seven years and you will find a use for it.

Soon got, soon spent.

Quickly come, quickly go.

VANITY

Pride goes before a fall.

Vanity of vanities; all is vanity.

All is vanity and vexation of spirit.

He walks as if balancing the family tree on his nose.

Every man has just as much vanity as he wants understanding.

Vanity is the quicksand of reason.

VICE

There is no vice without virtue.

What's vice today may be virtue tomorrow.

Judge not that ye be not judged.

Vices in one part of the world may be virtues in another.

The road to vices is not only smooth, but steep.

No man ever arrived suddenly at the summit of vice.

VISION

Where there is no vision, the people perish.

What we think, others materialise.

Even the wasted smoke is not traceless in the skies.

Vision is the art of seeing things invisible.

VICTORY

How beautiful is victory, but how dear!

The race is not to the swift, nor battle to the strong.

VIRTUE

Virtue is the strong stem of man's nature.

The only reward of virtue is virtue.

Virtue is health, vice is sickness.

Some rise by sin and some by virtue fall.

All great virtues bear the imprint of self-denial.

Virtue is its own reward.

Sermons in stones and good in everything.

One's outlook is a part of his virtue.

Virtue is like a rich stone, best plain set.

All bow to virtue and then walk away.

Love virtue rather than fear sin.

VOICE

The voice of the people is the voice of God.

God hears those whom nobody hears.

If we could solve all the mysteries of the universe, we would be co-equal with God.

Every drop of ocean shares its glory, but is not the ocean.

W

WAGES

The wages of sin are death.

The labourer is worthy of his hire.

Be content with your wages.

The wage of discontentment is more discontentment.

WANT

Rather want less, than have more.

He is richest, whose wants are the fewest.

The greedy are always needy.

Only the poor can give much, because they want little.

Knock and it shall be opened unto thee.

How few our real want and how vast our imaginary ones!

The fewer our want, the nearer we resemble the gods.

WAR

War is a strange alchemist and in its hidden chambers are such forces and powers brewed and distilled that they tear down the plans of the victorious and the vanquished alike.

War is the negation of truth and humanity.

He who uses violence or rules others, who drinks intoxicants or seizes the goods of others is a Kafir.

War is the science of destruction.

War never leaves a nation, where it found it.

Offence is the best defence.

Might is right.

Everything is fair in love and war.

The ballot is stronger than the bullet.

War hath no fury like a non-combatant.

Rumours of wars are as bad as wars.

England expects every man to do his duty.

England has no permanent friends and no permanent enemies.

A bad peace is worse than war.

Cannon shots begin from pin-pricks.

Peace hath its victories no less renowned than war.

WEALTH

If wealth is lost, nothing is lost;
If health is lost, something is lost;
If character is lost; everything is lost.

The wealthy man is a slave of his wealth.

True wealth is health.

Some money you earn for yourself, the rest for your government.

Some money you earn for yourself, the rest for others.

Surplus wealth is a sacred trust.

The extravagant robs his heir; the miser robs himself.

You collect cup by cup but God pours out the whole kettle.

When God gives, he pours through the roof.

Where wealth accumulates, men decay.

Wealth either serves or enslaves the possessor.

It is easier for a camel to go through the eye of a needle, than for a rich man to enter the kingdom of God.

All wealth is the product of labour.

Get rich quickly.

Riches certainly make themselves wings.

He that maketh haste to the rich, shall not be innocent.

No man ever became suddenly rich.

Fortune favours fools.

Pluck is the best luck.

WELFARE STATE

A welfare state must provide its citizens against hazards of unemployment, sickness, old age and death.

WEATHER

When two Englishmen meet, their first talk is of the weather.

Fair weather cometh out of the north.

In the year of snow.

Fruit will grow.

Summer is acumen in.

A single swallow does not make summer.

WEST

Go west, young man and grow up with the country.

East is East and West is West.

East or West, home is the best.

East or West you may roam.
There is no place like home.

Go West and come East.

Wisdom travels from East to West and from West to East again.

WICKEDNESS

Wickedness is weakness.

Nobody is born a wicked man.

Wickedness proceeds from the wicked.

There can be no wickedness without virtue.

Wives are youngmen's mistresses, companions for middle age and old men's nurses.

WINE

Even a priest will accept a free cup of wine.

There is a devil in every berry of the grape.

WIFE

No life without wife.

An undutiful daughter will prove an unmanageable wife.

He knows little, who tells his wife, all he knows.

Every man who is high up, loves to think that he has done all himself: and the wife smiles and lets it go at that.

WILL

Where there is a will, there is a way.

There is nothing good or evil, save in the will.

Not my will, but thine be done.

One man can take a horse to water, but twenty cannot make him drink.

WISDOM

Wise men learn more from fools than fools learn from wise men.

Repentance is the beginning of wisdom.

A wise enemy is better than a foolish friend.

In much wisdom is much grief.

A word to the wise is enough.

The words of the wise are as goads.

It is easy to be wise after the event.

Never advise anybody to go to war or to marry.

Some are weather-wise, some are otherwise.

The wisest are the simplest.

Great men are not always wise.

Penny wise, pound foolish.

The price of wisdom is above rubies.

The fear of the lord is the beginning of wisdom.

A wise man knows not many things.

The highest wisdom has but one science-the science the whole-the science explaining the whole creation and man's place in it.

WISH

If wishes were horses, beggars would ride.

The wish is father to the thought.

If men can halve their wishes, they can double their achievements.

WIT

Brevity is the soul of wit.

WONDER

No wonder can last more than three days.

Wonder grows where knowledge fails.

WOMAN

Woman's hell is old age.

A woman's guess is much more accurate than a man's certainty.

Women always have mental reservations.

The society of women is the foundation of good manners.

One boy is more trouble than a dozen girls.

Frailty, thy name is woman.

Ingratitude, thy name is woman.

No matter how hard a man may labour, some woman is always in the background of his mind. She is the one reward of virtue.

Generally the woman chooses the man, who will choose her.

Women dress to please men and displease other women.

When a woman surrenders, it's because she has won.

Next to the wound, what women make best is the bandage.

There is no load heavier than a light woman.

A woman is a delusion men like to hug.

WOOING

Men are April when they woo, December when they wed.

Marriage is a romance in which the hero dies in the first Act.

Speak low if you speak love.

WORDS

Fair words butter no parsnips.

Let thy words be few.

How forcible are right words.

Work is work if you're paid to do it and it's pleasure if you pay to be allowed to do it.

Let no man deceive you with vain words.

Words are feminine; deeds are masculine.

In the beginning was the Word and the Word was with God and the Word was God.

Sticks and stones may break my bones, but words will harm me never.

WORK

Go to the ant, thou sluggard! Learn her ways and be wise.

Better wear out than rust out.

Workers of the world, unite!

Better work without wages than not to work at all.

All work and no play will make Jack a dull boy.

The labourer is worthy of his hire.

Light is the task when many share the toil.

WORLD

This is the best world, that we live in,
To lend and to spend and to give in,
But to borrow, or beg, or to get a man's own,
It is the worst world, that ever was known.

This world's a bubble.

Nothing is sure in this world, except death and taxes.

The nations are as a drop in a bucket.

WRONG

Two wrongs do not make a right.

To err is human; to forgive, divine.

The poor are always in the wrong, if not wronged.

Rich man's wrong is poor man's right.

The wrong always seems the more reasonable.

Physical strength can never permanently withstand the impact of spiritual force.

WORSHIP

Work in the workshop is worship.

WORTH

The game is not worth the candle.

A bird in hand is worth two in the bush.

Worth is more important than birth.

Breed is stronger than pasture.

Aim at quality, rather than quantity.

WRITING

The pen is mightier than the sword.

If you wish to be a writer, write.

Think much, speak little and write less.

YOUTH

There is a great difference between a young man looking for a situation and one looking for work.

Ruthless youth makes rueful age.

Youth will be served.

In youth we learn; in age we understand.

Forty is the old age of youth; fifty is the youth of old age.

Keep true to the dreams of the youth.

Young in mind, young in body.

Age, I abhor thee; Youth, I adore thee.

Young men soon give and soon forget affronts.

Old age is slow in both.

Our object in the construction of the state is the greatest happiness of the whole and not that of any one class.

Z

ZEAL

It is good to be zealously affected always in a good cause.

Let zest and zeal be your pulse and feel.

FAMOUS PROVERBS

Every dog has its day.

Life is short, art is long.

Slur is stronger than sword.

Do good, have good.

Health is wealth.

Too many cooks spoil the broth.

Speech is silver, silence is gold.

Constant dripping wears a stone.

Murder will be out.

A man is known by the company he keeps.

Clothes make the man.

Do not put off till tomorrow, what you can do today.

Breed is superior to birth.

A friend in need is a friend indeed.

Money is honey.

Nothing succeeds like success.

Borrowing is sorrowing.

Man does not live by bread alone.

What cannot be cured, must be endured.

Truth triumphs.

Change is the law of nature.

Haste makes waste.

Where there is a will, there is a way.

Time is money.

Care kills the cat.

Might is right.

Honesty is the best policy.

Do as you would be done by.

As you sow, so shall you reap.

Faith is the staff of life.

Courtesy pays.

Life is a bubble.

Danger is the spice of life.

Let sleeping dogs lie.

Water always runs down.

Pride goes before a fall.

Anger blows out of the lamps of the mind.

Man is mortal.

A little knowledge is a dangerous thing.

Where ignorance is bliss, it is folly to be wise.

An ounce of pluck is worth, a ton of luck.

An example is better than precept.

Crime never pays.

The handsome is that handsome does.

Eat, drink and be merry for tomorrow, we die.

Give the devil his due.

Easy come, easy go.

Love is the light of life.

Too much familiarity breeds contempt.

Each man for himself and devil take the hindmost.

Fortune favours fools.

Some time to work, some time to play.

Do not kill the hen, that lays golden eggs.

Pages survive the ages.

The race is for the swift, the battle is for the strong.

Look before you leap.

Do your best and leave the rest (to God).

Even for the best swimmer, some river may be too wide.

An empty brain is a devil's workshop.

Rome was not built in a day.

While in Rome, do as the Romans do.

A wise enemy is better than a foolish friend.

Trust breeds trust.

Many a true word is spoken in jest.

He laughs best, who laughs last.

Birds of a feather flock together.

Like father, like son.

Love is God.

Ill-gotten ill-spent.

The world is a mirror of the mind.

Two heads are better than one.

Those who live in a glass house, must not throw stones at others.

Love begets love.

In every cloud, there is a silver lining.

Laughter is the best medicine.

Keep your feet warm and head cool.

Masses are big babes.

Follow the golden mean.

Necessity is the mother of invention.

Coming events cast their shadow before.

One man's meat is another man's poison.

It takes two to make a quarrel.

The mills of God grind slow, but they grind exceedingly small.

An empty vessel makes much noise.

A stitch in time saves nine.

Brevity is the soul of wit.

Believe not each accusing tongue.

Some rise by sin, some by virtue fall.

He lacks most, who longs most.

Two of a trade seldom agree.

Many talk like Robinhood, who never shot with a bow.

If the sky falls, we shall catch larks.

A black sheep spoils the whole flock.

He gives thrice, who gives in a trice.

A rolling stone gathers no moss.

To understand others, you need only to look closely into your own heart.

Two great talkers will not travel far together.

Almost every man knows how to earn, but not one in a million knows how to spend.

Time once gone can never be recalled.

An empty door will tempt a saint.

Wolves may lose their teeth, but not their tempers.

There is many a slip between the cup and the lip.

Good wine needs no bush.

The pot calls the kettle black.

I smell a rat.

How long can you escape the inevitable?

First deserve, then desire.

A fat purse never lacks friends.

Borrowed garments never fit well.

A drowning man catches a straw.

Beggars cannot be choosers.

A great ship needs deep waters.

All are not saints that go to church.

All covet, all lose.

As you sow, so shall you reap?

Death devours the lamb, as well as the sheep.

Cut your coat according to your cloth.

Every bean has its black.

His bread is buttered on both sides.

Man proposes, God disposes.

When all people say you are an ass, it is time to bray.

Society moulds a man.

Death makes no distinction between persons.

It is hard to sit at Rome and fight with the Pope.

Every cobbler to his task.

Give him an inch and he will have all.

He can never be God's martyr that is the devil's servant.

He was born with a silver spoon in his mouth.

Every rise hath a fall.

Every potter praises his own pot.

A diamond cuts diamond.

A contented mind is a continual feast.

Puff not against the wind.

Christmas comes but once a year.

Forbidden fruits are sweet.

He is a soul among the prophets.

Money begets money.

Virtue is its own reward.

It is no use to be wise after the event.

Let not your left hand know what your right hand does.

A blind man is no judge of colours.

Curst cows have short horns.

I talk of chalk and you talk of cheese.

Distance lends enchantment to the view.

East or West, home is best.

A little leak will sink a great ship.

Vows made in storms, are forgotten in calms.

Danger past, gods forgotten.

It is a silly fish that is caught twice with the same bait.

A bitter jest is the poison of friendship.

Appearances are deceptive.

Every cock fights best on his own dunghill.

Do not blow your own trumpet.

Everything looks pale on the jaundiced eye.

He that runs fast will not run long.

A pimple has grown upon an ulcer.

You have been hiding your light under a bushel.

Hungry dogs will eat dirty pudding.

Hunger is the best sauce.

The wish is father to the thought.

A clear conscience fears no accusation.

A soft answer turneth away wrath.

Man lives on hope.

Blood is thicker than water.

Blows will answer blows.

Crows are none the white being washed.

Deceit will not succeed long.

Misfortune overtook his first adventure.

Fools rush in, where angels fear to tread.

Ignorance of law is no excuse.

Prophets are not respected in their own country.

How piggish of a worthless fellow to assume consequential airs.

Embark first, debark last.

An ounce of example is better than a ton of precept.

Every spring is followed by autumn.

The nearer the church, the farther from God.

A word and a stone let go cannot be recalled.

A priest goes no further than the church.

As is the priest, so is the clerk.

Tell the truth and shame the devil.

The jackal's evil fate drives him towards the village.

Where the king is, there is the court.

As the old cock crows, so crows the young.

Bare words buy no barley.

A close mouth catches no flies.

Usage beats grammar.

Seat a poor man on a horse's back and he will ride to a fall.

An old dog will learn no tricks.

The older the goose, the harder to pluck.

My foot my tutor.

He will never set the Thames on fire.

No crow, no crown.

Grief is the canker of the heart.

He that is giddy, thinks the world turns round.

Argus at home, but a mole abroad.
Tomorrow will take care of itself.
Strike the iron while it is hot.
In a calm sea, every man is pilot.
He who seeks, shall find.
'Pretty pussy' will not feed a cat.
Spend and God will send.
A full purse never lacks friends.
Knaves starve not in the land of fools.
Blind of sight, called Mr. Bright.
Money for money and interest besides.
The deeper the well, the cooler the water.
Good mind, good find.
To swallow a camel and strain at a gnat.
A nod to the wise and rod for the foolish.
To fry one is one's own grease.
The wearer alone knows where the shoe pinches.
A sinful hand makes an ailing heart.
A burnt child dreads the fire.
The butcher looked for his knife when he had it in his mouth.
Loveliness requires not the foreign aid of ornament.
The morning shows the day.

A good name is better than riches.

A fool and his money are soon parted.

What is a pound of butter among a kennel of hounds?

Who diggeth a pit shall fall therein.

I ask for bread and you give me stone.

You cannot get oil from stones.

I am stout, you are stout, who will carry the dirt out.

The cheap buyer takes bad meat.

A wise foe is better than a foolish friend.

Man is the slave of habits.

Man is mortal.

The grave is the general meeting place.

He is over head and ears in debt.

They agree like pickpockets in a fair.

When a good cheer is lacking, the friends will be packing.

Do not count your chickens before they are hatched.

Small wit great boast.

It never rains but it pours.

Appetite is a universal wolf.

It is a foolish sheep that makes the wolf his confessor.

The first day a man is a guest, the second, a burden, the third, a pest.

Absence increases love, presence strengthens it.

As you make your bed, so you must lie on it.

If the blind lead the blind, both shall fall into the ditch.

None so deaf as those who will not hear.

Believe not all that you see nor half what you hear.

The good is often the enemy of the best.

Evil communications corrupt good manners.

It is good sometimes to hold a candle to the devil.

Set a thief to catch a thief.

Old habits persist.

Half a loaf is better than no bread.

The best is yet to be.

He is the best general, who makes the fewest mistakes.

Two blacks do not make a white.

A honeyed tongue and a heart of gall.

To run with the hare and hunt with the hound.

Much cry, little wool.

Like masters, like servant.

In for a penny, in for a pound.

New lords new laws.

You cannot make Mercury of every log.

The boaster and the liar are cousins germane.

A cow knows not the value of her tail, till she has lost it.

Rome was not built in a day.

Those who live in glass houses, should not throw stones at others.

There are men and men and every stone is not a gem.

It is an ill bird that fouls its own nest.

Everybody considers his own geese swans.

Silent men like silent waters are deep and dangerous.

Better give the wool than the whole sheep.

Uneasy lies the head that wears the crown.

A little pot is soon hot.

Business may be troublesome, but idleness is pernicious.

A crooked stick will have a crooked shadow.

MODERN PROVERBS

If business is good, you should advertise; if business is bad, you have got to advertise.

I expect to pass through this world but once. Any good therefore that I can do, or any kindness that I can show to any fellow creature, let me do it now. Let me not defer or neglect it, for I shall not pass this way again.

A lawyer must first get on, then get honour and then get honest.

Life is a jigsaw puzzle with most of the pieces missing.

Good luck is a lazy man's estimate of a worker's success.

Optimism: A cheerful frame of mind that enables a tea kettle to sing though in hot water up to its nose.

An optimist sees an opportunity in every calamity; a pessimist sees a calamity in every opportunity.

Youth is blunder, manhood struggle, old age regret.

Genius is one-tenth inspiration and nine-tenth perspiration.

Nobody ever became great by chance; nothing ever was achieved by sheer luck.

As rivers that run slowly have always the most mud at their bottom, so a stolid stiffness in the constant course of a man's life is a sign of thick bed of mud at the bottom of his brain.

No man can be a pure specialist without being in the strict sense an idiot.

Have a place for everything and have everything in its place.

Learn something of everything and everything of something.

Eat to live, not live to eat.

A pessimist is one who feels bad when he feels good for fear he'll feel worse when he feels better.

A bachelor is one who enjoys the chase, but does not eat the game.

A banker is a man who lends you an umbrella when the weather is fair and takes it away from you when it rains.

God and a soldier, all people, adore. In times of war, but not before; And when war is over and all things are righted, God is neglected and an old soldiers lighted.

Just one fine day does not make a spring.

Fools dream, wise men plan and act.

A bachelor is a souvenir of some woman who found a better one at the last minute.

Marriage is a lonely island surrounded by an ocean of expenses.

FAMOUS LINES OF LEADERS

Non-violence is a cult of the brave.

Mahatma Gandhi

Freedom is my birthright and I shall have it.

Lokmanya Tilak

Love must conquer hate, for hate cannot conquer itself.

Swami Vivekananda

Democracy is a government of the people, by the people, for the people.

Abraham Lincoln

The only thing we have to fear is fear itself.

F.D. Roosevelt

V for victory.

Winston Churchill

I will rather have violence than cowardice masquerading as non-violence.

Mahatma Gandhi

I do not want to harm the meanest insect, but it would give me the greatest pleasure if all the black-marketers were hung by the neck till dead.

Jawaharlal Nehru

It is weakness to yield on vital principles.

Jawaharlal Nehru

Seek ye first political freedom and all things shall be added unto thee.

Kwame Nkrumah

H is easy to hate, but healthy to love.

Dr. Radhakrishnan

East is East and West is West.
And never the twain shall meet.

Kipling

When a diplomat says yes, he means perhaps; when he says perhaps he means no; when he says no he is no diplomat.

Anonymous

A diplomat is a man who remembers a lady's birthday but forgets her age.

Anonymous

Discontentment is the cause of all progress.

Anonymous

A people at war with a mighty foreign Government cannot indulge in any festivities.

Sardar Patel

Every nation has a right to self-determination.

Dr. Munro

Marriage is a matter of mutual misunderstanding.

Oscar Wilde

It is dangerous to be too good.

George Bernard Shaw

A gentleman is man, who can disagree without being disagreeable.

Anonymous

Do not do unto others as you would that they should not do unto you. Their tastes may not be the same.

G.B. Shaw

A politician thinks of the next elections; a statesman thinks of the next generation.

Anonymous

Politics is a devil's game.

Anonymous

In Heaven, an angel is nobody in particular.

G.B. Shaw

Do not put off till tomorrow, what you can do the day after.

Oscar Wilde

Human history is in essence, a history of ideas.

H.G. Wells

Eat, drink and be merry, for tomorrow ye die.

William Gilmore Beymer

The world must be made safe for democracy.

Woodrow Wilson

Art is I; science is we.

Claude Bernard

To get into the best society nowadays, one has either to feed people, amuse people or shock people.

Oscar Wilde

Simplicity of character is no hindrance to the subtlety of intellect.

John Viscount Morley

Swaraj (political independence) has no meaning until it can annihilate the yawning gulf between the haves and the have-nots.

Maulana Azad

The theory of communism may be summed up in one sentence: Abolish all private property.

Karl Marx

Communism possesses a language which every people can understand-its elements are hunger, envy and death.

H. Fine

Workers of the world, until! You have nothing to lose except your chains.

Lenin

From each according to his ability, to each according to his needs.

Louis Blang

Capital is dead labour that vampire like lives only by sucking living labour and lives the more the more labour it sucks.

Karl Marx

Before the revolution, we too had sex. But not now.

Alexei Adzhubei

Lands may be confiscated from those, who do not cultivate them.

Chanakya

I do not believe that we should insist that anyone, who is not with us, is against us.

Dean Rusk

I wanted to change the world, but I have found that the only thing one can be sure of changing is, oneself.

Aldous Huxle

Submission to God is the only balm that can heal the wounds he gives.

Emmons

A welfare state must provide its citizens against hazards of unemployment, sickness, old age and death.

Dr. S. Radhakrishnan

Ignorance does not cease to be ignorance because of repetition among persons, no matter how numerous.

Mahatma Gandhi

A nation lives in its present on its past for the future.

Surendra Nath Banerjee

A deceiver deceives, only himself.

Mahatma Gandhi

Tears hinder sorrow from becoming despair.

Remember there can be no happiness for anyone unless it is won for all.

Sir Jagdish Chandra Bose

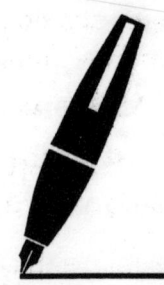

IDEAS OF GREAT AUTHORS

So much to do, so little done.

Cecil Rhodes

There is no education like adversity.

Disraeli

Good counsel has no price.

Mazzini

America is a tune. It must be sung together.

G.S. Lee

Breed is stronger than pasture.

George Eliot

When angry count four.

Mark Twain

The ideas that follow are of great authors, which have now become proverbial and many people just do not know who coined them.

Let us do or die.

Burns

Beware the fury of a patient man.

John Dryden

Well begun is half done.

Horace

It is the beginning of the end.

Tollyrand

A bird in hand worth two in the bush.

Cervantes

Divided rule and foreign rule are both unadulterated evils. Divided rule perishes owing to mutual hatred, partiality and rivalry. Foreign rule on the other hand impoverishes the country and carries off its wealth or treats it as a commercial article.

Chanakya

Borrowing is not much better than begging.

Lessing

Men willingly believe, what they wish.

Julius Caesar

The worst national rule is better than the best foreign rule.

Swami Dayanand

Beware of the man of one book.

Disraeli

A boy is, of all beasts, the most difficult to control.

Plato

None but the brave, deserve the fair.

John Dryden

Better is half a loaf, than no bread.

Heywood

Birds of a feather, flock together.

Minsheu

God blesses us every one.

Charles Dickens

Laws die, books never.

BulwerLytton

Don't quarrel with your bread and butter.

Swift

Know on which side, your bread is buttered.

Heywood

The fewer the words, the better the prayer.

Luther

The British are a nation of shopkeepers.

Samuel Adams

The business of America is business.

Calvin Coolidge

The nature of America is swindling.

August Rebel

Whispers cut honest throats.

Scott

A cat may look at a king.

John Heywood

Caution is the eldest child of wisdom.

Victor Hugo

The Revolutions are not made, they come.

Wendell Phillips

The old order changeth yielding place to the new.

Tennyson

It is a wise child that knows his own father.

Homer and Shakespeare

Child is father of the man.

William Shakespeare

To be like Christ, is to be a Christian.

William Penn

I am a citizen not of Athens, but of the world.

Socrates

Hasten slowly.

Augustus Caesar

Little boats should keep to the door.

Franklin

The people are the city.

William Shakespeare

Cleverness is not wisdom.

Euripides

Common sense is very uncommon.

Horace Greeley

Comparisons are odious.

Archbishop Bolardo

Sweep is revenge-specially to women.

Lord Byron

Freedom is my birthright and I shall have it.

Tilak

Shoemaker, stick to your last!

Pliny

Silence is one great art of conversation.

Hazlitt

Society is built upon trust.

Southe

Self-conquest is the greatest of victories.

Plato

Knowledge is power.

Francis Bacon

I must be cruel only to be kind.

William Shakespeare

It is darkest before the dawn.

Thomas Fuller

What a day may bring, a day may take away.

Thomas Fuller

Call no man happy till he is dead.

Aeschylus

Nothing can happen more beautiful than death.

Walt Whitman

Debt is the worst poverty.

M.G. Lightwer

Whatever is worth doing at all, is worth doing well.

Lord Chesterfield

Give me the ready hand, rather than the ready tongue.

Garibaldi

Heaven never helps the man, who will not help himself.

Sophocles

Despair is the conclusion of fools.

Disraeli

Here is the devil-and-all to pay.

Cervantes

Disappointment is the nurse of wisdom.

Sir Boyle Roche

Do not disturb the sleeping dog.

Allegri

Every dog must have his day.

Swift

Eat to please yourself, but dress to please others.

Franklin

Water is the only drink for a wise man.

Thoreau

England expects every man to do his duty.

Nelson

The proof of the pudding is in the eating.

Cervantes

Schoolhouses are the republican line of fortifications.

Horace Mann

Man is his own worst enemy.

Cicero

To err is human, to forgive divine.

Alexander Pope

Coming events cast their shadows before.

Campbell

Can there be bliss when all that lives must suffer? Shall thou be saved and hear the whole world cry?

Gautama Buddha

Ideals are like stars; you may not succeed in touching them with your hands. But, like the sea-faring man on the desert of waters, you choose them as your guides and in following them you will reach your destiny.

Carl Schurz

Ignorance does not cease to be ignorance because of repetition among persons, no matter how numerous they are.

Mahatma Gandhi

There is a point at which by its persistence beyond bearing capacity error over-reaches itself and thereby may come our deliverance from it.

C. Rajangopalachari

Every torment I have inflicted, every sin I have committed, every wrong I have done, I carry the consequence thereof with me. Strange, that I came with nothing in this world and now I go away with this stupendous caravan of sin.

Aurangzeb

Idleness wastes the sluggish body, as water is corrupted unless it moves.

Ovid

A word spoken in wrath is the sharpest sword; covetousness is the deadliest poison; passion is the fiercest fire: ignorance is the darkest night.

The Buddha

A friend in the market is better than money in the chest.

Thomas Fuller

Nothing has such power to broaden the mind at the ability to investigate systematically and truly, all that comes under the observation in life.

Marcus Aurelius

Pampered vanity is a better thing, perhaps than starved pride.

Joanna Baille

To the sinful man sin appears sweet as honey. The fool who knows his foolishness, is wise at least so far. But a fool who thinks himself wise, is a foul indeed.

The Buddha

If you wish to draw tears from me, you must first feel pain yourself.

Horace

A compromise is a bargain; a transaction of interests between two conflicting powers; it is not a true reconciliation. True reconciliation proceeds always by a mutual comprehension, leading to some sort of intimate oneness.

Sri Aurobindo

Justice is often pale and melancholy; but gratitude, her daughter, is constantly in the flow of spirits and the bloom of loveliness.

W.S. Landor

It is a smaller thing to suffer punishment than to have deserved it.... the punishment can be removed, the fault will remain forever.

Ovid

He who talks much of his happiness, summons grief.

George Herbert

One whose mind roams in search of outward beauty and grandeur; who is unable to keep mastery control over his senses; who eats impure food: who is lazy and lacking in moral courage: ignorance and sorrow overpower him just as the gale shatters the sapless tree.

Misfortunes come on wings and depart on foot.

G.G. Bohn

The misuse of great powers is no argument against their right use. To go back is impossible: the attempt is always, indeed, an illusion.

Sri Aurobindo

And he gave it for his opinion, that whoever could make two ears of corn or two blades of grass to grow upon a spot of ground where only one grew before, would deserve better of mankind; and do more essential service to his country than the whole race of politicians put together.

Jonathan Swift

Three things are known only in three places; valour, which knows itself only in war; wisdom, only in anger and friendship only in need.

Emerson

Indeed, adversity, suffering, may often be regarded as a reward to virtue rather than as a punishment for sin, since it turns out to be the greatest help and purifier of the soul struggling to unfold itself.

Sri Aurobindo

Even as justice to be justice has to be generous, generosity in order to justify itself has got to be strictly just.

Mahatma Gandhi

He only is great man, who can neglect the applause of the multitudes and enjoy himself, independent of favour.

Richard Steek

Hasty and adventurous schemes are at first view flattering, in execution difficult and in the issue disastrous.

The Gita is the universal mother. She turns away nobody. Her door is wide open to anyone who knows. A true votary of the Gita does not know what disappointment is. He ever swells in perennial joy and peace that passeth understanding.

Mahatma Gandhi

He that is proud eats up himself; pride is his own glass his own trumpet, his own chronicle: and whatever praises itself but in the deed, devours the deed in the praise.

WilliamShakespeare

Good manners and soft words have brought many a difficult thing to pass.

Sir John Vanburgk

The real ornament of woman is her character, her purity. Metal and stones can never be real ornaments. Real ornamentation lies not in loading the body with metal and stones, but in purifying the heart and developing the beauty of the soul.

Mahatma Gandhi

I do not know what I may appear to the world, but to myself I seem to have been only a boy playing on the seashore and diverting myself in now and then, finding a smoother pebble or a prettier shell than ordinary, whilst the great ocean of truth lay all undiscovered before me

Issac Newton

Spiritual development ought to be given the first place in the choice for marriage. Service should come next, family considerations and the interest of the social order should have the third place and mutual attraction or "love" the fourth and last place. This means that "love" alone where the other four conditions are not fulfilled should not be held as a valid reason for marriage. At the same time, marriage, where there is no love, should equally be ruled out even though all the other conditions are fully complied with.

Mahatma Gandhi

Many persons might have attained to wisdom, had they not assumed that they already possessed it.

Seneca

The young man who has not wept is a savage and the old man who will not laugh, is a fool.

Santayana

Love of God is the only Love that is higher than a Mother's Love. All others are lower.

Swami Vivekananda

When you can use, the lightning is better than cannon.

Napoleon

Society is a masked ball, where everyone hides his real character and reveals it by hiding.

Emerson

Life is a continuous struggle of man against man, of man against his surrounding, a struggle on the physical, intellectual and moral plane out of which new things take shape and fresh ideas are born.

Jawaharlal Nehru

Essentially, I am interested in this world, in this life, not is some other world or a future life.

Jawaharlal Nehru

The less men think, the more they talk.

Montesquieu

Said the pot to the kettle, "Get away, blackface!"

Cervantes

A man of action, forced into a state of thought, is unhappy until he can get out of it.

Galsworthy

Truth is not only vitiated by falsehood; may be equally outraged by silence.

Amien

MORE PROVERBS

In English, the stock of proverbs is very large, covering the whole field of human activity. Experiences about social, political and domestic affairs, about agriculture, trade, morality and religion are all enshrined in these proverbs and stock-sayings. Although in standard literary writings they are very specially used, in conversational English they abound profusely and their use gives colour, force and vividness to our speech. It is always interesting to study the story or image which is hidden behind a proverb and amplify it in our own words. The following proverbs that are given below will facilitate ready reference.

A bad workman quarrels with his tools. (People who are not able to do a thing properly attribute their failure to everything, but not to the true cause, which is their own want of ability).

A bird in hand is worth two in the bush. (A small benefit which, we actually enjoy is better than a great one inexpectation).

A burnt child dreads the fire. (One who has once got into trouble by anything will avoid it ever afterwards. The same fact is expressed by the proverb: "The scalded dog fears cold water".)

"There is often more true spiritual force in a proverb than in a philosophical system."

Thomas Carlyle

A guilty conscience needs no accuser. (If man has really done something wrong, he will betray it by his behaviour even though no one may suspect it or charge him with it.)

A liar should have a good memory. (If he tells one lie, he will have to tell many others to hide that lie; and if he does not remember all the lies he invents, he may contradict them and so betray himself).

A drowning man will catch at a straw. (People who are reduced to extreme circumstances will resort to even the most unlikely means to get out of them).

A little pot is soon hot. (Little persons are commonly passionate and provocable).

A penny saved is a penny gained. (To avoid squandering, a penny has the same effect as earning a penny).

A pin a day is a goat a year. (A pin is of very small value, but to throw away a pin everyday is the same as throwing away a goat a year).

A rolling stone gathers no moss. (A person who constantly leaves one appointment for another, will never become a well-to-do or rich man).

A stitch in time saves nine. (If we remedy an evil in time, it will prevent a great deal of trouble afterwards).

A great cry and little wool. (A good deal of noise or fuss is often made about a thing, which is really of no importance at all.)

A little leak will sink a great ship. (We should not despise a danger, because it appears small or insignificant).

A fool's bolt is a soon shot. (Simpletons cannot wait for the proper time, but waste their resources in random endeavours.)

A tree is known by its fruit. (The character of a person is judged by his actions and not by his words).

A hedge between keeps the friendship green. (As a hedge between two farms imparts some greenness to the land, in the same way, slight aloofness between two friends keeps their friendship fresh and constant).

A sleeping fox catches no poultry. (A man who is careless and invigilant gains nothing).

A man without purpose is a ship without a rudder. (As a ship without rudder is always exposed to the mercy of winds, in the same way, a man who has no clear or decisive goal in life is more likely to fail than succeed).

A good presence is a letter of recommendation. (A happy and graceful disposition helps a man in any interview as much as a letter of recommendation).

A rotten sheep infects the whole flock. (A single bad man corrupts the whole company in which he lives, i.e., 'A single sinner sinks the boat'.)

A contented mind is a continual feast. (Contentment is the greatest good we can hope for in life. It does not bring wealth but it banishes the desire of it, which is much more valuable. Contentment is natural wealth, luxury is artificial poverty).

A bald head is soon shaved. (A simple and innocent man is easily deceived).

All are not saints that go to church. (We should judge a man not by his outward conduct but by his inward character).

An old bird is not to be caught with chaff. (An experienced man or one with his experience about him, is not to be deluded by humbug. The reference is to throwing chaff instead of bird-seed to allure birds).

An angry man opens his mouth and shuts his eyes. (A man who is in angry state of mind is governed by passions and loses all self-control).

An Englishman's home is his castle. (This is a common saying, meaning that every English man is as secure in the privacy of his own house as if he were a baron or lord in his castle; the officers of government will not enter his home, but allow him to remain the undisputed master there).

An empty bag cannot stand upright.s (A man devoid of truth and the force of reason cannot succeed in a discussion).

Barking dogs seldom bite. (People who threaten a great deal, seldom put their threats into practice).

Beggars must not be choosers. (When we seek a favour, we must take what we get and not be discontented with it).

As you sow so you shall reap. (We must abide by the consequences of our own acts).

As are the gods, so are the worshippers. (The character of the people is formed by their leaders).

Beggars bleed and rich men feed. (The rich prosper because the poor starve).

Better be alone than in bad company. (It is better not to have any friends or associates at all than to have such as will corrupt us).

Better short of pence than short of sense. (It is better to be a man of knowledge and commonsense than to be one of money or wealth).

By the street of by-and-by one arrives at the house of never. (By postponing a thing little by little a man is never able to do it).

Caesar's wife must be above suspicion. (The reputation of a great man's wife must be without blame; hence any one who moves in select circles must be above reproach).

Catch the bear before you sell his skin. (Never be sure of a thing, till you have actually got it).

Better to wear out than to rust out (Doing something is better than doing nothing).

Birds of the same feather flock together. (Persons of the same character or temperament, generally associate together).

Blood is thicker than water. (Kinship is stronger than friendship for water evaporates, but blood does not).

Creaking doors hang the longest. (Sickly persons very often outlive the strong.)

Cut your coat according to your cloth. (We must spend according to our income).

Desperate diseases require desperate remedies. (Extreme measures are necessary to put down an evil, for which ordinary means are inffectual).

Even Aesop had no remedy for superstition. (There is no cure for doubt and disbelief).

Every cock crows on its own dunghill. (Everyone can boast in his own home; the same as 'Every dog is a lion at home').

Example is better than precept. (Preaching by action is more effective than preaching by words. We imitate another's conduct more readily than we follow his advice).

Fast bind, fast find. (Take proper precaution in regard to any property and you will not lose it).

Don't hallo before you are out of the wood. (Don't rejoice too soon or feel happy till all danger is over).

Eat to live, but not live to eat (Do not be a glutton, but eat only what is necessary for your sustenance).

Empty vessels make most noise. (None are more apt to boast than those who have the least worth. The deepest stream flows with least noise).

First weigh then say. (Consider well before you act; the same as 'Look before you leap').

Forgiveness is the noblest revenge. (The way of being revenged upon a man who injures you is to forgive him).

God helps those who help themselves. (A man should do all he can and leave the result to God).

God tempers the wind to the shorn lamb. (God softens the affliction of a sufferer or lightens the burden of the poor and helpless).

Good wine needs no bush. (A good article will make itself known without being advertised. The reference is to the old custom of pushing up an ivy-bush before the doors of inn and taverns. The ivy was sacred to Bacchus, the god of wine).

Handsome is that handsome does. (The really handsome person is not one who has a pretty face, but one who acts handsomely i.e., liberally or generously).

Hell is paved with good intentions. (Then are many in hell who resolve to reform, but do not carry out their good resolutions. The proverb means that it is not sufficient to make good resolutions, but we must carry them out).

He lacks most, who longs most. (He who has numerous wants, never has his wishes gratified, the more he desires, the more he is dissatisfied).

Grasp all, lose all. (By trying to get too much you may lose even what you have).

Habit is second nature. (What we are accustomed to do as readily as if it were natural to us: custom makes all things easy).

Honey is not for the ass's mouth. (Gentle words are wasted on unreasonable persons; also good things are not meant for those who are incapable of understanding their value).

Hunger is the best sauce. (A hungry man will not be particular about the quality of the food he gets to eat. His hunger will make even the worst food tasteful.

If things were to be done twice, all would be wise. (Men learn wisdom by experience; and the evil results of an error once made teach us to avoid it afterwards).

If the sky falls, we shall catch larks. (A person unwilling or incompetent to do something, does not admit his own weakness but makes his performance depend upon such conditions as are impossible).

It is never too late to mend. (There is always time to improve if we only set about it in earnest).

It is not the cowl that makes the monk. (Everyone who wears a cowl-hood of a monk is not a monk. We should not judge people's real character by their outward appearance).

It is hard to sit in Rome and fight with the Pope. (We cannot quarrel with those upon whom we depends).

It never rains, but it pours. (Fortunes like misfortunes not come alone. When we are favoured with fortune, we are favoured to the full).

Ill news travels apace. (Bad news spreads very fast).

It is an ill wind that blows nobody good. (It is a disastrous event or overwhelming misfortune that brings no good to anyone).

Light gains make a heavy purse. (Small profits and quick return is the best way of gaining wealth).

Love me, love my dog. (If you love me, you will have to love all whether pleasant or unpleasant, that belongs to me).

Make hay while the sun shines. (Avail yourself of opportunities when they occur).

Man proposes, God disposes. (We may begin any enterprise we please, but its success depends on God's will).

Many kiss the child for the nurse's sake. (There are many who show us sympathy and love for achieving their own private ends).

Many talk like Robinhood who never shot with a bow. (Many boast of bravery without ever having done anything brave).

Mice will play when the cat is away. (A servant will enjoy freely when the master is away).

Money makes the mare go. (Much can be accomplished with the power of money).

Necessity has no law. (Circumstances sometimes compel us to do things which we do not like to do).

Need makes the naked man run. (Under the pressure of need, a man does all kinds of unexpected things; the same as 'Need knows no law').

Necessity is the mother of invention. (When a want is keenly felt, some plan will certainly be devised to supply it).

No gains without pains. (If we want to gain any profit or advantage, we must work for it and not leave it to fortune).

No man can serve two masters. (It is a Biblical saying meaning that man can serve either God or Mammon (God of wealth) but not both at the same time).

Opportunity makes the thief. (Even an honest man may yield to strong temptation. The Italians say, "Where a chest lies open, a righteous man may sin." The proverb warns us against throwing temptation in the way of servants etc. by leaving boxes open and so on).

One swallow does not make spring. (The reference is to the migration of swallows, which leave England on the approach of winter and return with Spring. The proverb means that one man alone cannot do the whole thing).

One slays, another pays. (The crime is committed by one and punishment is borne by another).

One beats the bush, another catches the hare. (One does the work, another enjoys the benefit).

No rose without a thorn. (There is no pleasure or enjoyment, which is entirely free from something painful or disagreeable).

Nothing venture, nothing have. (There can be no gain unless there is also some risk of loss: we must risk a little to gain much).

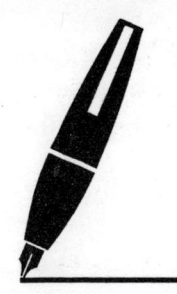

MISCELLANEOUS

"yes is a world
& in this world of
yes live
(skilfully curled)
all worlds"

~ e.e. cummings

"Savor. To appreciate fully; enjoy or relish: I want to savor this great moment of accomplishment. [From Latin sapere, to taste.]"

"A man is as unhappy as he has convinced himself he is."

~ Seneca

"A problem can not be solved with the same consciousness that created it."

~ Albert Einstein

"A stumbling block to the pessimist is a stepping-stone to the optimist."

~ Eleanor Roosevelt

"A verse from the Veda says, 'What you see, you become.' In other words, just the experience of perceiving the world makes you what you are. This is a quite literal statement."

~ Deepak Chopra

"A warrior must cultivate the feeling that he has everything needed for the extravagant journey that is his life. What counts for a warrior is being alive. Life in itself is sufficient, self-explanatory and complete. Therefore, one may say without being presumptuous that the experience of experiences is being alive."

~ Carlos Castaneda

"A warrior never worries about his fear."

~ Carlos Castaneda

"A warrior takes responsibility for his acts, for the most trivial of acts. An average man acts out his thoughts and never takes responsibility for what he does."

~ Carlos Castaneda

"As the physically weak man can make himself strong by careful and patient training, so the man of weak thoughts can make them strong by exercising himself in right thinking."

"Become a possibilitarian. No matter how dark things seem to be or actually are, raise your sights and see possibilities - always see them, for they're always there."

~ Norman Vincent Peale

"Believe in yourself! Have faith in your abilities! Without a humble but reasonable confidence in your own powers, you cannot be successful or happy."

~ **Norman Vincent Peale**

"Circumstances—what are circumstances? I make circumstances."

~ **Napoleon Bonaparte**

"Conceit is an unusual disease; it makes everyone sick but the one who has it."

~ **Unknown**

"Confidence is directness and courage in meeting the facts of life."

~ **John Dewey**

"Convictions are more dangerous enemies of truth than lies."

~ **Friedrich Nietzsche**

"Could we change our attitude, we should not only see life differently, but life itself would come to be different. Life would undergo a change of appearance because we ourselves had undergone a change of attitude."

~ **Katherine Mansfield**

"Determine that the thing can and shall be done and then we shall find the way."

~ **Abraham Lincoln**

"Do not let what you cannot do, interfere with what you can do."

~ John Wooden

"Don't go around saying the world owes you a living. The world owes you nothing. It was here first."

~ Mark Twain

"Don't waste your time on jealousy. Sometimes you're ahead; sometimes you're behind. The race is long and in the end, it is only with yourself."

~ Mary Schmich

"Doubts ... often beget the facts they fear."

~ Thomas Jefferson

"Enjoy yourself—it's later than you think."

~ Guy Lombardo

"Every exit is an entry somewhere."

~ Tom Stoppard

"Everything good and bad comes from your own mind. To find something beyond the mind is impossible."

~ Bodhidharma

"Everything hangs on one's thinking."

~ Seneca

"False words are not only evil in themselves, but they infect the soul with evil."

~ Socrates

"Fame or integrity: which is more important? Money or happiness: which is more valuable? Success or failure: which is more destructive? If you look to others for fulfillment, you will never truly be fulfilled. If your happiness depends on money, you will never be happy with yourself. Be content with what you have; rejoice in the way things are. When you realize there is nothing lacking, the whole world belongs to you."

~ Lao-tzu

"Finally, brothers, whatever is true, whatever is noble, whatever is right, whatever is pure, whatever is lovely, whatever is admirable—if anything is excellent or praiseworthy—think about such things."

~ Jesus

"Find the best in others."

~ Unknown

"Men are anxious to improve their circumstances, but are unwilling to improve themselves."

~ James Allen

"For every difficulty that supposedly stops a person from succeeding, there are thousands who have had it a lot worse and have succeeded anyway. So can you."

~ Brian Tracy

"Getting used to our blessings is one of the most important nonevil generators of human evil, tragedy and suffering."

~ Abraham Maslow

"God turns you from one feeling to another and teaches by means of opposites, so that you will have two wings to fly, not one."

~ Mevlana Rumi

"Hardy folks don't run from change; they exult in its challenges."

~ Unknown

"He is a letter to everyone. You open it. It says, 'Live!'"

~ Mevlana Rumi

"He who binds to himself a joy

Does the winged life destroy;

But he who kisses the joy as it flies

Lives in Eternity's sunrise."

~ William Blake

"Hold on to the centre and make up your mind to rejoice in this paradise called life."

~ Lao-tzu

"I am burning. If anyone lacks tinder, let him set his rubbish ablaze with my fire."

~ Mevlana Rumi

"I am more and more convinced that our happiness or our unhappiness depends far more on the way we meet the events of life, than on the nature of those events themselves."

~ Karl Wilhelm Von Humboldt

"I care not so much what I am to others as what I am to myself."

"I have been driven many times upon my knees by the overwhelming conviction, that I had nowhere else to go. My own wisdom and that of all about me seemed insufficient for that day."

~ **Abraham Lincoln**

"I have known a great many troubles, but most of them never happened."

~ **Mark Twain**

"I keep my ideals, because inspite of everything I still believe that people are really good at heart."

~ **Anne Frank**

"I love men who can smile in trouble, who can gather strength from distress and grow brave by reflection."

~ **Thomas Paine**

"I think luck is the sense to recognize an opportunity and the ability to take advantage of it. Everyone has bad breaks, but everyone also has opportunities. The man who can smile at his breaks and grab his chances gets on."

~ **Samuel Goldwyn**

"I want to seize fate by the throat."

~ **Ludwig van Beethoven**

"If I have lost confidence in myself, I have the universe against me."

~ **Ralph Waldo Emerson**

"If I have the belief that I can do it, I shall surely acquire the capacity to do it even if I may not have it at the beginning."

~ Mahatma Gandhi

"If you are distressed by anything external, the pain is not due to the thing itself but to your own estimate of it; and this you have the power to revoke at any moment."

~ Marcus Aurelius

"If you look at your life one way, there is always cause for alarm."

"If you would perfect your body, guard your mind."

~ James Allen

"Imaginary obstacles are insurmountable. Real ones aren't."

~ Barbara Sher

"Imagination was given to man to compensate him for what he is not and a sense of humor was provided to console him for what he is."

~ Unknown

"In the depth of winter, I finally learned that within me, there lay an invincible summer."

~ Albert Camus

"Inspiration may be a form of super-consciousness, or perhaps of sub-consciousness—I wouldn't know. But, I am sure it is the antithesis of self-consciousness."

~ Aaron Copland

"It is easy in the world to live after the world's opinion; it is easy in solitude to live after our own; but the great man is he who in the midst of the crowd keeps with perfect sweetness the independence of solitude."
~ Ralph Waldo Emerson

"It is not a lucky word, this name impossible; no good comes of those who have it so often in their mouths."
~ Thomas Carlyle

"It is not the failure of others to appreciate your abilities that should trouble you, but rather your failure to appreciate theirs."
~ Confucius

"It's kind of fun to do the impossible."
~ Walt Disney

"It's not what you look at that matters, it's what you see."

"Judgement comes from experience and great judgment comes from bad experience."
~ Bob Packwood

"Let no feeling of discouragement prey upon you and in the end, you are sure to succeed."
~ Abraham Lincoln

"Little by little, a person becomes evil, as a water pot is filled by drops of water...

Little by little, a person becomes good, as a water pot is filled by drops of water."
~ Buddha

"Luke: I can't believe it. Yoda: That is why you fail."

~ Yoda

"Man often becomes what he believes himself to be. If I keep on saying to myself that I cannot do a certain thing, it is possible that I may end by really becoming incapable of doing it. On the contrary, if I shall have the belief that I can do it, I shall surely acquire the capacity to do it, even if I may not have it at the beginning."

~ Mahatma Gandhi

"Many of the truths we cling to, depend greatly on our point of view."

~ Obi-Wan Kenobi

"May you never forget what is worth remembering; Or remember what is best forgotten."

~ Unknown

"Men are born soft and supple; dead, they are stiff and hard. Plants are born tender and pliant; dead, they are brittle and dry. Thus whoever is stiff and inflexible is a disciple of death. Whoever is soft and yielding is a disciple of life. The hard and stiff will be broken. The soft and supple will prevail."

~ Lao-tzu

"Men do not attract that which they want, but that which they are."

~ James Allen

"Minds are like parachutes - they only function when they are open."

"More than those who hate you, more than all your enemies, an undisciplined mind does greater harm."

~ Buddha

"Nothing can stop the man with right mental attitude from achieving his goal; nothing on earth can help the man with the wrong mental attitude."

~ Thomas Jefferson

"Nothing is a waste of time, if you use the experience wisely."

~ Auguste Rodin

"Nothing is at last sacred, but the integrity of your mind."

~ Ralph Waldo Emerson

"Once a man worries, he clings to anything out of desperation; and once he clings he is bound to get exhausted or to exhaust whomever or whatever he is clinging to. A warrior-hunter, on the other hand, knows he will lure game into his traps over and over again, so he doesn't worry."

~ Carlos Castaneda

"Our life is shaped by our mind; we become what we think. Suffering follows an evil thought as the wheels of a cart follow the oxen that draws it.

Our life is shaped by our mind; we become what we think. Joy follows a pure thought like a shadow that never leaves."

~ Buddha

"Pain is a relatively objective, physical phenomenon; suffering is our psychological resistance to what happens. Events may create physical pain, but they do not in themselves create suffering. Resistance creates suffering. Stress happens when your mind resists what is...The only problem in your life is your mind's resistance to life as it unfolds."

~ Dan Millman

"Pain is inevitable. Suffering is optional."

~ Dalai Lama

"People only see what they are prepared to see."

~ Ralph Waldo Emerson

"People seem not to see that their opinion of the world is also a confession of character."

EXERCISE:

MATCH THE FOLLOWING:

A bad workman ...

A bird in the hand ...

A fool and his money ...

A friend in need ...

A miss ...

A rolling stone ...

A small leak ...

A stitch in time ...

Absence ...

All's well that ...

... gathers no moss

... are soon parted

... is a friend indeed

... is as good as a mile

... can sink a great ship

... saves nine

... ends well

... blames his will clutch at a straw

... makes the heart grow fonder

... is worth two in the bush

ANSWERS:

A bad workman blames his will clutch at a straw

A bird in hand is worth two in the bush

A fool and his money are soon parted

A friend in need is a friend indeed

A miss is as good as a mile

A rolling stone gathers no moss

A small leak can sink a great ship

A stitch in time saves nine

Absence makes the heart grow fonder

All's well that ends well

An apple a day ...

Another man's grass ...

Any time ...

As you make your bed, ...

Beauty is in the eye ...

Better half a loaf than ...
Better late than ...
Birds of a feather ...
Charity ...
Children should be seen ...
Cut your coat ...
Discretion ...
Don't count your chickens ...

... keeps the doctor away
... is always greener
... means no time
.... so must you lie on it
... of the beholder
.... than no bread
... never
... flock together
.... begins at home
.... and not heard
.... according to your cloth
.... is the better part of valour
.... before they are hatched

ANSWERS:

An apple a day keeps the doctor away

Another man's grass is always greener

Any time means no time

As you make your bed, so must you lie on it

Beauty is in the eye of the beholder

Better half a loaf, than no bread

Better late, than never

Birds of a feather flock together

Charity begins at home

Children should be seen and not heard

Cut your coat according to your cloth

Discretion is the better part of valour

Don't count your chickens, before they are hatched